Sri Ram Charit Manas

DIAMOND POCKET BOOKS PRESENTS

RELIGION & SPIRITUALITY BOOKS

B.K. Chaturvedi
- *Gods & Goddesses of India 150.00
- *Shiv Puran 95.00
- *Vishnu Puran 95.00
- *Shrimad Bhagvat Puran .. 75.00
- *Devi Bhagvat Puran 75.00
- *Garud Puran 95.00
- *Agni Puran 95.00
- *The Hymns & Orisons of Lord Shiva (Roman) 30.00
- *Sri Hanuman Chalisa (Roman) 30.00
- *Pilgrimage Centres of India 95.00

S. K. Sharma
- *The Brilliance of Hinduism 95.00
- *Sanskar Vidhi (Arya Samaj) 95.00

Dr. B.R. Kishore
- *Hinduism 95.00
- *Rigveda 60.00
- *Samveda 60.00
- *Yajurveda 60.00
- *Atharvveda 60.00
- *Mahabharata 60.00
- *Ramayana 60.00
- *Supreme Mother Goddess Durga (4 Colour Durga Chalisa) 95.00

Manish Verma
- *Fast & Festivals of India .. 95.00

Manan Sharma
- *Buddhism (Teachings of Buddha) 95.00
- *Universality of Buddha 95.00

Anurag Sharma
- *Life Profile & Biography of Buddha 95.00
- *Thus Spake Buddha 95.00

Udit Sharma
- *Teachings & Philosophy of Buddha 95.00

Dr. Bhojraj Dwivedi
- *Annual Horoscope 2003 (12 Zodiac Signs in one book) .. 95.00
- *Hindu Traditions & Beliefs 150.00

Dr. Giriraj Shah
- *Glory of Indian Culture 95.00

F.S. Growse
- *Mathura & Vrindavan, The Mystics Land of Lord Krishna .... 495.00 (Coloured photoes)

R.P. Hingorani
- *Chalisa Sangrah (Roman) .. 40.00

Acharya Vipul Rao
- *Srimad Bhagwat Geeta (Sanskrit & English) 75.00

Dr. Bhavansingh Rana
- *108 Upanishad (In press) ... 150.00

Chakor Ajgaonkar
- *Realm of Sadhana (What Saints & Masters Say) 30.00

Dr. S.P. Ruhela
- *Fragrant Spiritual Memories of a Karma Yogi 100.00

Yogi M.K. Spencer
- *Rishi Ram Ram 100.00
- *Oneness with God 90.00

Eva Bell Barer
- *Quiet Talks with the Master 60.00

Joseph J. Ghosh
- *Adventures with Evil Spirits 80.00

K.H. Nagrani
- *A Child from the Spirit World Speaks 10.00

Religious Books in Hindi, English & Roman
- *Sanatan Dharm Pooja 95.00
- *Sudha Kalp 95.00
- *Shiv Abhisek Poojan 25.00
- *Daily Prayer (Hindi, English French, Roman) 25.00
- *Sanatan Daily Prayer 25.00

Acharya Vipul Rao
- *Daily Prayer 10.00

Dr. Shiv Sharma
- *The Soul of Jainism 125.00

Prof. Gurpreet Singh
- *The Soul of Sikhism 125.00
- *Ten Masters 60.00

Order books by V.P.P. Postage Rs. 20/- per book extra. Postage free on order of three or more books, Send Rs. 20/– in advance

DIAMOND POCKET BOOKS (P) LTD.
X-30, Okhla Industrial Area, Phase-II, New Delhi-110020.
Phones : 51611861 - 865, Fax : (0091) -011- 51611866, 26386124

Sri Ram Charit Manas

Translated by
S.P. Ojha M.A. English
Principal
**Saraswati Shishu Mandir, Haidargarh
Barabanki (U.P.)**

DIAMOND POCKET BOOKS
X-30, Okhla Industrial Area, Phase - II
New Delhi - 110 020

No part of this book may be reproduced or transmitted in any form or by any means electronic or mechanical including photocopying or recording or by any information storage and retrieval systems without permission in written from **Diamond Pocket Books (P) Ltd.**

© Publisher
ISBN : 81-7182-071-9

Published by	:	DIAMOND POCKET BOOKS (P) LTD. X-30, Okhla Industrial Area, Phase - II New Delhi - 110 020
	:	✆ : 011-51611861-65 Fax : 011-26386124 E-mail : mverma@nde.vsnl.net.in Website : www.diamondpocketbooks.com
First Edition	:	2003
Price	:	Rs. 95/-
Laser Typesetting	:	R. S. Prints ✆ : 26857488, 26512856
Printed by	:	Adarsh Printers, Navin Shahdara, Delhi-110032

Sri Ram Charit Manas
Translated by S.P. Ojha   Price : 95/-

Manas At A Glance

Sri Ram Charit Manas is not just a book. It is a holy scripture which has been revered and respected down the ages. Perhaps there is hardly any home, where Ram Charit Manas is not found.

Ram Charit Manas, as all know, narrates the story of Lord Rama, the incarnation of Lord Vishnu. The vital difference between Ram Charit Manas and Ramayan is that the former was authored by Tulsidas in Awadhi language while the latter was written by Valmiki in Sanskrit. Despite this, the essence remains same. The idea is to propagate the social and religious message to the discerning readers.

Lord Rama's life has been envisioned as an illustrated example and Sri Ram Charit Manas endeavours to make people realize this and live a fair and just life.

श्री राम परिवार को नमस्कार

रामं रामानुजं सीतां, भरतं भरतानुजं।
सुग्रीवं वायु सूनं च, प्रणमामि पुनः पुन॥
चरितं रघुनाथस्य, शतकोटि प्रविस्तरम्।
एकैकमक्षरं पुंसां, महापातक नाशनम्॥

Rāmaṃ Rāmānujaṃ Sītāṃ, Bharataṃ Bharatānujaṃ.
Sugrīvaṃ Vāyu Sūnaṃ Ca, Praṇamāmi Puna: Puna..
Caritaṃ Raghunāthasya, Śatakōṭi Pravistaram.
Ēkaikamakṣaraṃ Puṃsāṃ, Mahāpātaka Nāśanam.

Meditation

I worship that supreme power who fulfils the wishes of his devotees. Whom *Brahma, Vishnu* and *Shiva* etc. are serving regularly. *Hanuman, Sugreeva* and *Bharat* with all the brothers are serving and worshipping, who is the ocean of pity. I touch the feet of that Lord Sri Ram who is *Shyam Sunder*, dressed in yellow, happy faced, and whose eyes are red like lotus.

Arati Sri Ramayan Ji Ki

Arati Sri Ramayan Ji ki,
Kirati Kalit Lalit siya piya ki
Gawat Brahmadik Muni Narad
balmiki vigyan visharad,
Sukh, sankadi shesh aru sharad,
varani Pawansut kirati neeki,
Arati Sri Ramayan Ji ki. (1)

Gawat Ved, Puran ashtadasha,
chhahoe shastra sab granthan ko ras,
Munijan dhan santan ko sarvas,
sar ansha sammat sabhi ki,
Arati Sri Ramayan ji ki. (2)

Gawat santat Sambhu, Bhawani,
Aru ghat sambhaw Muni viggyani,
Byas aadi kavi braj bakhani,
Kag-Bhushundi Garun ke hiya ki,
Arati Sri Ramayan ji ki. (3)

Kali mal harani vishaya ras fiki,
Subhag singar mukti yubati ki,
Dalan rog bhawa moori amiya ki,
Tat Mat sab vidhi Tulsi ki,
Arati Sri Ramayan ji ki. (4)

Kind Request

The learned readers are well aware that the main copy of Sri Ram Charit Manas was written by the honourable Goswami Tulsidas, the great poet of Hindi dialect, which is probably not available anywhere. On the basis of Sri Ram Charit Manas published by Geeta Press, Gorakhpur, I have tried my best to present the summary of Sri Ram Charit Manas in a prose form. Several questions may strike your mind as to why I have translated it in English language? The question may be true, no doubt. But as far as my thinking is concerned, the present mentality of the society, especially the so called high-educated families are in favour of speaking in English. They like to read the books in English. They also want to express their ideas in English language. Whenever you are travelling by bus or by the train, you may see some learned people reading English magazines or English novels in their hands. They feel great pride in reading English books.

To know more about the English writers, thinkers, philosophers and scientists is very good. Because now-a-days English has become an international language. But we ought to know much more about our ancestors, about our Lords and Gods and Goddesses. We should never forget that India has been Vishwa Guru. It is said, that when all the countries of the world were crawling on their knees, India had shown them the path of wisdom, culture and civilization. This was the case of our country. The culture of Mohenjodaro and Harappa, the University of Takshila and Nalanda, the pillar of Ashok Ashtambha all indicate towards our glorious past.

I am not in favour to compel the learned readers, that they should not get the knowledge of English as a language or as a literature. But I request our readers to know themselves first, then something else. Hindi is our national language. Mahabharat, Ramayan, Bhagwat Gita, Puran and Upanishads are the body of Hindi language. But Sri Ram Charit Manas is the soul of Hindi language. Manas is the pious and religious book of Hindus. This book has been written in Awadhi dialect. A man of little knowledge can read and recite the lines of Manas in a sweet tone. He can understand the sense of Manas very easily. Even the illiterate easily follow the theme of Manas.

In this materialistic age, man has no time to study the lengthy religious books, because they are time-consuming. So I have prepared a brief sketch of Sri Ram Charit Manas as a mental tonic for those persons, who are fond of studying the religious book in a short time. After a study of four-five hours, one can come to the conclusion of Sri Ram Charit Manas. We can know a lot about the ideal life of Sri Ram, within a short time.

My heart is full of gratitude for those gentlemen, who have given their precious advise and co-operation. At last, I will request the learned readers to excuse me for the mistakes because "To err is human, to forgive is divine." In this way, the thing of God is presented to God.

Introduction

There are several religions in the world. Every religion has its own pious book which tells us a lot about the qualities of that very religion. Bible is the only-book of Christianity. Quran is the only book of Islam but in Hindu religion there are many pious books like Ramayan, Bhagwat Gita, Puran, Upnishads, Vedas, Mahabhrata, Satyartha Prakash and Sri Ram Charit Manas etc. These books tell us more about the goodness and greatness of Indian culture and civilization. They also tell us about our Sanatan Hindu Dharam. Sri Ram Charit Manas is the soul of Indian culture. Manas has been composed by Goswami Tulsidas, the great poet of Hindi language. It is said that Goswami Tulsidas was Trikaldarshi. He had a great knowledge of past, present and future. His sayings were true, are true and will be true for all the times to come. Actually Goswami Tulsidas was not a mere poet, but was also a great social reformer. He roamed throughout the whole country and studied the real problems which were prevailing in the society. These problems were illiteracy and untouchability. There was a high wall among the rich and the poor. These problems were main hindrance in the development and integration of the country. He found that all people are in a deep sleep. They were helpless from all sides. Such type of mentality was rooted in common people that they may not think for their progress. Every one was helpless and undone.

So Goswami Tulsidas wrote this great epic Sri Ram Charit Manas in Awadhi dialect to awaken the Indian culture and civilization. Through this great epic, "Manas", Tulsidas has tried to preach the people about the ideals of our Lord Sri Ram. Fact is that, Ram is present in every particle of the universe. He, the almighty has taken birth on this earth from time to time for the protection of the good and for the destruction of the bad. We may not take Him as a great king of Ayodhya. We should not take Him as the elder son of king Dashratha the great king of Ayodhya. But we all the citizens of India consider Him as our Lord. Thus we can say that Sri Ram was not for an age but for all the times to come. In this way His ideals are immortal. His guidelines will show the path of truth and wisdom to our coming generations for centuries.

Sri Ram Charit Manas the pious book of our Indian culture is highly respected in every home of the Indians. It is regarded in huts in the same way as it is regarded in the palace of the President. This pious book is divided into seven parts (Khands). These Khands are call Kand. They are Bal Kand, Ayodhya Kand, Aranya Kand, Kishkindha Kand, Sunder Kand, Lanka Kand and Uttar Kand. In this pious book, there are nine main steps and thirty substeps. These steps, kands and substeps help us in studying this book in a proper manner. The words and sentences of this book are so simple that a common man or a lesser qualified person can also read and understand its sense very easily. Even an uneducated peasant can also understand and recite the lines of manas. Sri Ram Charit Manas is written in Awadhi dialect, which is spoken by common people. It is written in Doha, Chopai, Soratha and Chhand. In the beginning of every kand, the shlokes of Sanskrit language are used to pray Lord Shiva and Parwati, Lord Ganeshji, Lord Sri Ram and Sita, Lord Vishnu and laxmi.

Whenever, we read or recite the lines of "Manas", we feel a great deal of pleasure in our hearts. Generally people call it Ramayan. You may get Sri Ram Charit Manas in every home of India. People feel grace that they have Ramayan in their houses. Some people read it regularly after taking bath at the time of meditation or worship. On some pious occasions people arrange the "Path" recitation of Manas for twenty-four hours. It is their faith, that Lord Sri Ram will fulfil wish of that person who arrange the "Path" of Manas for twenty-four hours.

If Tulsidas would have not sung "Manas" the Ramayan, who would have shown us the right path of religion for the progress of the country. Goswami Tulsidasji says that in Kaliyug, the name of Sri Ram is the only base of life. The name of Sri Ram is superior than Lord Sri Ram Himself.

कलियुग केवल नाम अधारा।
सुमिरि सुमिरि नर उतरहिं पारा॥
कहँ लगि कहौं मैं नाम बड़ाई।
राम न सकहिं नाम गुण गाई॥
Kaliyug keval naam adhara
Sumiri sumiri nar utarahim para.
Kahn lagi kahon mein naam badaii
Ram na sakahin naam gun gayi.

The great poet of Hindi literature Sri Veni says that in absence of Goswami Tulsdas, who would have developed the love in the stone hatred people? Paying his homage in the feet of Goswami Tulsidasji, poet "Veni" further says soundly that who would have taken us across the Bhawasagar, if Tulsi would have not sung the Ramayan.

भारी भव सागर उतारतो कौन पार।
जौ पै यह रामायण तुलसी न गावतो।
Bhari bhav sagar utarto koun par,
Jou pai yah Ramayan Tulsi na gawato.

About Sri Ram Charit Manas, Goswami Tulsidas himself says that I have sung this song in the feet of Lord Ram for self satisfaction.

'स्वान्तः सुखाय तुलसी रघुनाथ गाथा'
"Swantah sukhaya Tulsi Raghunath gatha."

Though Goswami Tulsidas wrote Sri Ram Charit Manas from self satisfaction point of view, but today it has become more lovable and honourable not only in Indian but throughput the whole world. Through Sri Ram Charit Manas, Goswami Tulsidas has tried to bring near the southern people to the northern people. He has shown the victory of truth on untruth. He has shown the victory of non-violence over violence. He has shown the victory of Aryan culture on Rakshas culture. There is a vivid description of the virtues of Lord Sri Ram. This is the reason that Lord Sri Ram establishes the statue of the Lord Shiva in Rameshwaram at the time of the advancement of their army towards Lanka. People from North India go to worship Lord Shiva in Rameshwaram. People from South India come to worship Lord Sri Ram in Ayodhya. Thus, they come in contact with the culture, customs, traditions, rituals, civilization and with our functions to each other in the whole country.

Ram, the ideal character of Tretayug is the main centre of this book. Every character of Sri Ram Charit Manas is ideal in itself. The character of Ram as an ideal king is worth praising. In Ram Rajya, people were leading a prosperous life. Every body was healthy, wealthy and wise. That why our Rashtrapita Mahatma Gandhi imagined for such a Ram Rajya in our country, where people will lead a pleasant life, where no body will die of hunger, where all will be leaned and well behaved, where religious people will guide the countrymen and where the constitution will be made on the ground of religion. Here I shall try to define the world religion, because at present people have a confusion about this word religion. The word religion means Dharam. Dharam means duty. The religion of the sun is to give heat for the welfare of all the creatures of the universe. If he does not do so, what will happen? Every thing in the world will go in ruins. The life will become impossible on the earth. In the same way if the moon, the stars do, human being should also follow their religions. Because the religion takes us towards bright future.

In Ram Rajya, King Sri Ram was following their religion, so there was prosperity in every sphere of life.

राम राज्य बैठे त्रैलोका, हर्षित भये गये सब सोका।
बयरू न कर काहू सन कोई राम प्रताप विषमता खोई॥
दैहिक दैविक भौतिक तापा, राम राज नहि काहुहि ब्यापा।
सब नर करहि परस्पर प्रीति, चलहि स्वधर्म निरत श्रुति नीति।
राम राज कर सुख सम्पदा, वरनि न सकहि ॰नीस सारदा॥

Ram Rajya bethey triloka,
harshit bhaye gaye sab soka.
Bayaru na kar kahoo san koie
Ram Pratap Vishamta khoie
Dahik davik bhotic tapa
Ram raj nahi kahuhi vyapa
Sab nar karahi paraspar preeti
chalahi swadharm nirat shruti neeti
Ram Raja kar sukh sampada,
varani na sakahi phanis sarda.

As an ideal brother, the behaviour of Ram with their brothers is remarkable one. He loved his brothers by heart and all the brothers loved him wholeheartedly. The behaviour of Lord Sri Ram with his brothers is an extra ordinary example of brotherhood in India. This was the reason that at the time of going to forest, Laxman followed their elder brother Sri Ram for his service, leaving aside the royal comfort of the palace. When Bharat came to know that obeying their father king Dashratha, Ram has gone to forest with his lovable wife Sita, he could not check himself. In this way Bharat went to meet Ram in Chittrakoot. Bharat tried his best and requested Sri Ram again and again to come back to Ayodhya, but failed. Sri Ram was firm on his determination. At last Bharat requested Sri Ram to give his wooden sandal. Ram agreed at this proposal. Bharat took the wooden sandal of Lord Sri Ram and seated it on the throne of Ayodhya. Bharat left all his princely dresses and began to live like a saint in the Nandi village.

> तेहि पुर बसत भरत बिनु रागा।
> चंचरीक जिमि चम्नक बागा॥
> Tehi pur barat Bharat binu raga
> Chancharik jimi chamnak baga.

Bharat stayed there in Nandi village upto the time of exile. For 14 years, he chanted the nome of Sri Ram.

The character of Ram as an ideal husband is also worth praising. When his beloved wife Sita follows Him to the forest Ram asks her not to go with him, because there were lots of trouble and pain in the forest. Even then Sita followed her husband and Ram had to agree with her. Sita requested Ram in such a way, which impressed Sri Ram too much. Sita said:

> जिय बिनु देह नदी बिनु बारी, तैसेइ नाथ पुरूष बिनु नारी।
> नाथ सकल सुख साथ तुम्हारे, सरद विमल विधु बदनु निहारे॥
> को प्रभु संग मोहि चितवनहारा, सिंघ बघुहि जिमि ससक सियारा।
> अस कहि सीय विकल भइ भारी, वचन वियोग न सकी संभारी।
> देखि दसा रघुपति जिय जाना, हठि राखे नहिं राखिहि प्राना॥

Jiyu binu deh nadi binu bari, tesaji nath purush Binu nari.
Nath sakal sukh sat tumhare, sarad vimal vighu badnu nihare.
Ko prabhu sang mohi chitvanhara, singh baghuhi jimi sasak siyara.
As kahi siya vikal bhai bhari, vachan viyog na saki sambhari.
Dekhi dasa raghupati jiya jana, hathi rakhe nahin rakhihi prana.

Sri Ram allowed Sita to go with him. In the forest Ram was always ready to protect his beloved wife Sita on every moment. Laxman his younger brother was also accompanying him in this matter. When Ravan the demon king of Lanka came in disguise and saw Sita alone he stole her away. As Ram came to know that someone has stolen Sita, he became very sad. Ram started to search for Sita with Laxman. Being Lord, Sri Ram wept in the forest for his wife as a common man of the world. He asked the trees and plants and wild animals in the forest about Sita.

> हे खग मृग है मधु कर श्रेनी, तुम्ह देखी सीता मृग नैनी।
> हमहि देखि मृग निकर पराहीए मृगी कहहिं तुम कह डर नाहीं॥
> तुम्ह आनन्द करहु मृग जाये, ये कंचन मृग खोजन आये॥
> Hey khag margh hay madhu kar shreni,
> Tumh dekhi sita mrugh naini.

Hamahi dekhi mragh nikar parahiye mraghi,
Kahahin tum kaha dar nahin.
Tum anand karahu mragh jaye,
Ye kanchan mragh khojan aaye.

Sri Ram has presented a better example of friendship. In the way to forest, when they were crossing the river Ganga, He became a friend of Kewat. When he was searching Sita in the forest he befriended Hanuman. With the help of Hanuman, Ram became friend with Vanar Raj Sugreevan also. In the way to the forest Ram served the injured vulture king Jatayu. Thus, Sri Ram has presented an ideal of friendship. He tried his best to abolish untouchability by his behaviour.

With the help of Sugreevan, when Sri ram came to know that the demon king of Lanka has stolen Sita, Jatayu had told Sri Ram the same thing. Ram became very angry at this. He took oath to abolish the demons and their cruelty from the earth. He raised his hands high in the sky and said:

निशिचर हीन करहु महिए भुज उठाइ प्रन कीन।
सकल मुनिन्ह के आश्रमन्ह, जाइ जाइ सुख दीन॥
Nishichr heen karhu mahiye, bhuj uthaye pran keen.
Sakal muninah ke ashramnah, jaai jaai sukh din.

Now Sri Ram arranged a huge army of Vanars and Bhaloos. A fierce battle took place and Ravan the demon king of Lanka was killed at last.

एक लाख पूत, सवा लाख नाती।
तेहि रावन घर, दिया न बाती॥
Ek lakh poot, sava lakh nati,
Tehi ravan ghar, diya na bati.

Thus, Ram came back to Ayodhya with his beloved wife Sita. On the sayings of a washerman Sri Ram left Sita in the forest at her pregnancy period. Though he send her out from the palace, but not from his heart. This was the reason that with the departure of Sita, Ram could not sleep soundly throughout his whole life.

In the forest, he became a friend of Sugreevan, Hanuman, Kewat, Jatayu and even Vibhishan also. Vanar Raj Sugreevan helped Sri Ram in searching out Sita and Sri Ram helped him to bring back his beloved wife from his elder brother Bali, who had kidnapped her. Hanuman was so much influenced with the behaviour of Lord Sri Ram that he became the life long servant and follower of Lord Sri Ram. This is the secret that Sri Ram is found in the heart of Hanuman, with Sita, and Hanuman is found in the feet of Lord Sri Ram. This is the excellency of friendship.

> प्रभु तरू पर कपि डार परए ते किय आप समान।
> तुलसी सीता नाथ सो॑ साहिब सील निघान॥
> Prabhu taru tar dar paraye te kiya aap saman.
> Tulasi Sita nath so sahib seel nidhan.

Ram as an ideal and obedient son is liked by all. At the time of coronation, when Sri Ram was going to become the king of Ayodhya, when all the family members of the palace were overjoyed, when the whole Ayodhya was decorated like a bride-groom to welcome their new King Lord Sri Ram, Kakeye the younger queen of King Dashratha, turned all the pleasure into sadness. She asked king Dashratha to send Sri Ram to the forest for fourteen years, when Ram came to know about this fact, he at once left all the princely dresses and without any hesitation he touched the feet of his parents and went to the forest. Thus, Sri Ram has paved the way for the coming generation to obey their parents without any ifs or buts.

Thus, Sri Ram Charit Manas teaches us that the character of Lord Sri Ram as an ideal son is an ideal for all the people. If the sons of today follow the footsteps of Lord Sri Ram, their parents will feel pleasure and they will do more for the welfare of their children. Discipline is the life of nation, in the same way discipline is the life of a family also. So if our coming generations will be obedient and disciplined, there is no doubt that our homes will be full of delight and prosperity.

Now a days, our coming generation is not going to follow the footsteps of Lord Sri Ram. This is the reason that our country is marching ahead towards beggary, social differences, untouchability, unemployment, illiteracy so on. This is my request to all the countrymen and specially with the coming generations that you please must follow the guide lines of Sri Ram Charit Manas. Only then, we may be able to give a complete social reform to our country. Sri Ram Charit Manas and its guide lines will prove as a milestone for the coming generations. In the present situation, when our social ideals are getting changed, there must be an ideal based on religious ground as an example before us. Sri Ram Charit Manas is sufficient in itself to give a proper guidance for the youths, who are the pillars of a nation. Only a strong person can make a strong nation. So, our youths must be strong by character, by body, by mind and by soul. In this connection, I request you all my learned readers to have faith and to follow the guide lines of Sri Ram Charit Manas. It will do good in every sphere of our life.

Chapter I
BAL KAND

First of all Goswami Tulsidas has prayed Ganeshji, the Lord of wisdom. We assume and it is our faith that whenever we start any great work, if we remember Lord Ganeshji he roots out all the difficulties of the way. He fulfils our aim. After praying Ganeshji, Tulsidas has prayed Lord Vishnu who is superior power for getting his mercy. And then he had bowed his head in the feet of his Guru, who is superior to all the gods.

गुरू ब्रह्मा गुरूर्विष्णु गुरूर्देवो महेश्वर:।
गुरू: साक्षात्परंब्रह्मा, तस्मै श्री गुरूवे नम:॥
गुरू पद नख सिख मनिगन ज्योति।
सुमिरत दिव्य दृष्टि हिय होती॥

Guru Brahma Guru Vishnu Guru Devo Maheshwarah,
Guruh Sakshatparambrahmah, tasmai Shri Guruve Namah.
Guru pad nakha sikha manigan jyoti,
Sumirat divya drishti hiya hoti.

Goswami Tulsidas further says that the name of Ram is more powerful and effective than Ram himself.

कहँ लागे करउँ मैं नाम बड़ाई।
राम न सकहिं राम गुण गाई॥
सबरी गीध सुसेवकन्हि, सुगति दीन्ह रघुनाथ।
नाम उघारे अमित खल, वेद विदित गुण गाथ।

Kahn lage karaun mein naam badaii,
Ram na sakahin ram gun gayi.
Sabari gigh susevkanhi, sugati dinh raghunath.
Naam ughara amit khal, ved vidit gun gath.

In this way if we try to find out the superiority between Ram and His name, the place of name will be superior than Ram. The name of Ram has been considered as mahamantra.

मंत्र महामणि विषम ज्वाल तै।
मेटत कठिन कुअंक भाल के॥

Mantra mahamani Vishnu Jwal te,
Metath kathin kuanka bhal ke.

Further we see that when Lord Shiva was discussing about the virtues of Lord Sri Ram, Parwatiji requested Lord Shiva to tell more about the greatness of Sri Ram. Lord Shiva says: Listen Parwati! I shall tell you why Ram took birth in the lap of Kaushilya. He told her that whenever sin grows and evil practices prevail in the society, when vedas, cows, brahamans, gods, and even Earth began to cry due to heavy load of sin, then the almighty and omnipresent God comes on the earth in several forms to console the ailing humanity.

जब जब होहिं धर्म कर हानी, बाढ़हि असुर अघम अभिमानी।
करहिं अनीति जाइ नहिं बरनी, सीदहि विप्र घेनु सुर घरनी॥
तब तब धरि प्रभु विविध सरीरा, हरहिं कृपा निधि सज्जन पीरा।

Jab Jab Hohin dharam kar hani, badahi aasur agham abhimani.
Karahi aniti jayi nahi barani, sidahi vipra ghenu sur gharani.
Tab tab ghari Prabhu vividh sarira, harahi kripa nidhi sajjan pira.

Once Rishi Narad cursed Lord Vishnu that inspite of being God and almighty you have to weep for the wife like me. Because you have not given me a chance to marry. Vishnu Bhagwan accepted the curse of Rishi Narad. Thus, when Lord Vishnu took birth in Treta Yug in Ayodhya as Ram, he suffered the pain of separation from his beloved wife Sita and wept also.

Manu and Satrupa were the first men to produce human generation. Once after a hard penance, both wife and husband achieved blessing from God, that God himself will take birth in their home. So on getting time, when Manu and Satrupa left this world Manu become the king Dashratha in Ayodhya and Satrupa became his queen Kaushilya. King Dashratha was very famous for his bravery. He was Chakrawarti Samrat. It is said that Indra, the king of gods himself used to give honour to king Dashratha. When king Dashratha grew old, he thought within himself, that he would die sonless. Because upto the fourth stage of his age he had no son. So he asked their minister Sumantra to call Shringi Rishi for Puttrashthi Yagya (पुत्रेष्ठि यज्ञ).

श्रवण समीप भये सित केसा, मनहुँ जरठ पन अस उपदेसा।
श्रृंगी ऋसिमहिं वसिष्ठ बोलावा, पुत्र लाभ सुभ यज्ञ करावा।

Shravan sameep bhaye sit kesa, manhu jarat pan As updesa
Shrangi risimnhin vashith bolava, putra labh subh Yagna karava.

With the effect of yagna, all the queens became pregnant. After Some time, Dashratha got four sons. They were named Ram, Laxman, Bharat, Shatrughan. When king Dashratha got the news he was very pleased.

दसरथ पुत्र जन्म सुनि काना।
मानहुँ ब्रह्मानन्द समाना॥
Dasrath putra janma skni kana,
Manahu brahmanand samana.

Here, I shall try to define Bramhanand. Bramhanand is a such type of pleasure, which is beyond description. It can be only felt. For example, if we give sweet to a dump man, he could only feels its sweetness, but if you ask him about its taste he cannot describe about its sweetness. Thus, Bramhanand is such a type of pleasure which can be achieved by devotion. This is not spiritual pleasure. This is a heavenly pleasure.

According to Sri Ram Charit Manas, when Ram took birth in Ayodhya, at that time all the gods came to Ayodhya to see their Lord Sri Ram. Because he was an extraordinary son. His mother Kaushilya was wonder-struck to see the whole universe in the mouth of Ram when he smiled.

देखरावा मातहि 'निज अदभुत रूप अनन्त।
रोम रोम प्रति लागहिं, कोटि कोटि ब्रह्माण्ड॥
Dekhrava matahi nij adhbhut roop anant,
Rom rom prati lagahin, koti koti brahmand.

Now the news spread in whole Ayodhya that God the almighty himself has taken birth in the form of Ram. The son of Dashratha is not an ordinary son, he is Lord Ram. So, hearing this news all the residents of Ayodhya were overjoyed. There was a great rush at the palace of Dashratha. Several types of donations were distributed to the brahamans, the poors and to those, who came there at that time. The king gave elephants, chariots, horses, gold, diamond and princely dresses to the people according to their wish. Dashratha satisfied everyone who came there at that time. And so people blessed the sons for a long and happy life.

Time passed. Now the king thought to name the four sons. So, he called Guru Vashistha to get consultation about their name, Guru Vashishtha named them Ram, Laxman, Bharat and Shatrughan on behalf of their virtues. It is our faith that the name of a man influences his personality. These sons were loved by the people of Ayodhya in the same way as the king and queen loved them.

> कौशलपुर वासी नर, नारि, वृद्ध अरू बाल।
> प्रानहुँ ते प्रिय लागहिं, सब कहुँ राम कृपाल॥
> Kaushalpur vasi nar, naari, vadh aru baal.
> Pranabhun te priya lagahn, sab kahun Ram krupal.

Once Rishi Vishwamitra thought that our Lord Sri Ram has taken birth in Ayodhya. This is a very good and golden time to go Ayodhya to see Ram. He did the same. Rishi Vishwamitra reached Ayodhya. King Dashratha welcomed him warmly. Vishwamitra stayed there for some time. When he became ready to go back to his ashram, he requested Dashratha to give Ram and Laxman to go to forest with him for the protection of the yagna from the demons. Hearing this king Dashratha became very sad. King Dashratha says:

> चौथेपन पायउँ सुत चारी, विप्र वचन नहिं कहेउँ विचारी।
> कहँ निशिचर अतिघोर कठोरा, कहँ सुन्दर सुत परम किसोरा॥
> Chauthepan payau sut chari,
> vipra vachan nahi kaheun vichari.
> Kah nishichar atighor kathora,
> kahn sunder sut param kishora.

King Dashratha was not in the mood to send his sons with Vishwamitra in the forest. But when his family and Guru Vashishtha advised Dashratha that it would be better by all sides for the all-round development of Ram and Laxman. You please let your sons go with vishwamitra. Now Dashratha was satisfied with the advice of Guru Vashishtha and Vishwamitra. Rishi took them to his ashram in the forest for the protection of the yagna.

When Sri Ram and Laxman reached, the ashram of Muni Vishwamitra, they were much pleased to see the natural scene of the forest. They began to live happily with their guru. Rishi Vishwamitra gave all types of education to Ram and Laxman in the ashram. Being almighty and omnipresent God, they learnt every thing very easily and in a short time. They became famous archers of their age.

One day, wandering in the forest when Ram saw the disturbance of the Rakshsas in the yagna of the Rishis, he killed them with little effort. Rishi vishwamitra became much pleased to see the supreme power of Sri Ram. Rishi Vishwamitra thought that he had succeeded in his aim. Ram and Laxman will fulfil his wish. Vishwamitra gave all types of weapons to Sri Ram and Laxman. In the morning Sri Ram said to Rishi Vishwamitra to do his yagna fearlessly, because I am ready to protect you by all means. As soon as the Rishis started their yagna, Demon Mareechi came with his army to create disturbance in the yagna. they began to throw bones and meat in the yagna. Then Sri Ram shot without point an arrow on Mareechi which took him across the seven seas. His whole of the army ran away. Now all the Rishies and Munies became very glad to see the extraordinary power of Lord Sri ram. The Rishies began to worship in the ashram fearlessly. Ram killed several demons in the forest.

After passing some time in the ashram, one day Rishi Vishwamitra asked Sri Ram and Laxman to go with him to see the swayambar of Sita which was arranged by Janak the great king of Janakpur. Ram and Laxman followed the Rishi Vishwamitra happily, because there was curiosity in their mind to see new things in Janakpur. On the way to Janakpur, they saw a stone it was the beautiful wife of the Rishi Gautam. Once Indra, the king of gods cheated Rishi Gautam, because he wanted to get his beautious wife Ahillya.

When Gautam Rishi came to know this very fact, he had been cheated by Indra and by his own wife. He cursed them both, Indra and his wife Ahillya. In this way his wife became stone. Actually this stone is Ahillya the beautious lady of Gautam Rishi. She is waiting for you for a long time. She wishes to get rid of this curse.

गौतम नारिश्राप वस, उपल देह घरि घीर।
चरन कमल रज चाहति कृपा करउ रघुवीर॥

Gautam naarishraap vas, upal deh ghari ghir.
Charan kamal raj chahit, Krupa karav Raghuvir.

So, please touch this stone by your feet, so that she may come back to her original form. Ram did the same. As Sri Ram touched his feet to the stone, at once the stone turned in to a beautious lady. Now Ahillya prayed Sri Ram many times. Taking the blessing of Lord Sri Ram she went away to her husband Gautam Rishi.

Now Sri Ram and Laxman started towards Janakpur with Rishi Vishwamitra. They reached near Janakpur and stayed in an ashram. The ashram was at a fine place. There was a very good natural scene nearby the ashram. When king Janak came to know about the reaching of Rishi Vishwamitra, he himself went there at the ashram and requested Rishi to come to the palace to bless his daughter Sita in the swayambar. Rishi Vishwamitra agreed at his request. King Janak took them to his kingdom and arranged all the necessary things for them.

One day Sri Ram asked his Guru that younger brother Laxman wants to see the kingdom of king Janak. If you please permit us to go there, we shall come back very soon. Hearing the polite and sweet words of Ram, Rishi smiled. He permitted them to go to see the city with Laxman. They went to see the city pleasantly. As soon as the two brothers entered the city of Janakpur, many boys were very happy to see them. They roamed in the city for some time. All the men and women of Janakpur were astonished to see such a beauty, because they had never seen such type of beauty before. Every one was amused to see Ram and Laxman. They went to that place also, where the swayambar was to be held. They watched the whole celebration minutely. After some time they came back to their Guru Vishwamitra.

On the other morning, after taking bath Guru Vishwamitra asked Ram and Laxman to bring some flowers. They went away in search of flower for worship.

> समय जानि गुरू आयसु पाई, लेन प्रसून चले दोड भाई।
> Samay jani Guru aayasu payi, len Prasoon chale dou bhai.

Searching the flower they reached near Pushpavatika of king Janak. The garde, was well decorated with different types of flowers by nature. The natural scene of the garden (Pushpavatika) was very charming and attractive. Sri Ram asked the gardener to let them allow to pluck and take some flowers for worship. The gardener agreed with the proposal of Sri Ram. Sri Ram and Laxman entered in Pushpavatika. Firstly, they walked in the garden to see the charming scene. As they were willing to take flowers, they heard an attractive sound in Pushpavatika from a corner. Some ladies were also entering the Pushpavatika from other side. Princess Sita the daughter to king Janak came there with her friends to worship goddess Gauri.

> कंकण किंकिनि नूपुर घुनि सुनि।
> कहत लखन सन राम हृदय गुनि॥
> मानहु मदन दुदुंभी दीन्ही।

मनसा विश्व विजय चह कीन्ही॥
Kankan kinkin nupur ghuni suni.
Kahat lakhan san Ram hriday guni.
Manuhu madan dundubhi dinhi.
Mansa vishwa vijay chah kinhi.

A friend of Sita saw Ram from a distance. She was wonder struck to see such a natural and extraordinary personality in Pushpavatika. She ran towards her companions. She told Sita about that. She asked Sita please come with me. At first you see such a extraordinary personality with me, then worship goddess Gauri.

बहुरि गौरिकर ध्यान करेहँ।
भूप किशोर देखि किन लेहँ॥
Bahuri gaurikar dhyan karehen.
Bhup kishor dekhi kin lehn.

Princess Sita did the same. She went towards that side where Ram and Laxman were standing. As she saw the charming and attractive beauty of Ram, she stood silently for a while. She closed her eyes and remembered about her ancient love with her Lord. Sita was much pleased with this happening. When her friends saw Sita in such a critical position, they asked her to go for worship goddess Gauri, because it was getting late. Thinking about the time, princess Sita Shivered of being late. At once they went to the temple of Devi Gauri, which was made in between the Pushpavatika. She worshipped Devi Gauri with flowers and requested her to fulfil her wish.

On the other hand when Ram saw Sita he was also astonished to see such a beautiful princess, Laxman awakened him from day dreaming and told that we have come here for taking flowers. He said that we are getting late. Our Guru Vishwamitra will be angry on us. Ram said to Laxman, well Laxman! You see that very gentle daughter of Janak is not an ordinary princess. Because being Ram, I am also much influenced with her. There is some extra quality in her that is why I am thinking again and again about the natural beauty of princess Sita. It seemed that the love of olden days was awakened in the heart of Ram. But he checked himself and asked Laxman to return back to their ashram. They took some pretty flowers and moved towards the ashram.

Next day, king Janak came there at the ashram of Rishi Vishwamitra. He requested them in a polite manner to visit the

Swayamber of their daughter Sita. Rishi Vishwamitra reached the place of Swayambar with their disciple Ram and Laxman. They watched the whole preparation and celebration of Swayambar very minutely. Vishwamitra praised king Janak for his fine preparation. They saw that several invited kings were seated on their seats according to their social status.

Rishi Vishwamitra sat on a grand seat with Ram and Laxman. Thousands of great kings were wonder-struck to see the charming, attractive, dominating and natural beauty of Sri Ram and Laxman. Even gods were present in the Swayambar of princess Sita in the sky on their vimans. We know it well that Sita was not an ordinary princess. We consider Sita as our mother. She is the mother of whole universe. She is the supreme power. She is the maker and destructor of all the creatures. So it was not unusual that gods were already fond of seeing the marriage ceremony of world's mother Sita.

As we know it well that, it was the condition of Swayambar that the person who will break the bow of Lord Shiva, he only will marry Sita. According to the declaration of king Janak, many kings tried to break the bow, but they failed. Nobody could move the bow even a single inch. Now king Janak became very hopeless. He was much disappointed at this. He thought that now our daughter Sita will remain unmarried. So he challenged all the kings of the Swayambar and said, I am very sad. I feel that there is no brave king on the earth. who could break this bow. Saying this tears appeared in the eyes of king Janak.

Seeing the critical position of king Janak and hearing his unbearable voice, Laxman became very angry. He shouted and said, if our guru and my elder brother Ram order me, I may lift the universe in my hand as a rubber ball. I can break the bow as a clay jug.

जौ राउर अनुशासन पाउँ, कन्दुक इव ब्रह्माण्ड उठाउँ।
काचे घट जिमि डारौं गेरी, सकउँ मेरू मूलक इव तोरी॥

Jo raur anushasan paun, kanduk iva Brahmand uthaun.
Kache ghat jimi daron phori, sakaun meru moolak iva tori.

Seeing the anger of Laxman, all the kings began to look here and there. They were afraid. Now Rishi Vishwamitra asked Sri Ram silently to break the bow. Ram stood from his seat. He touched the feet of their Guru Vishwamitra. Sri Ram marched towards the bow. As he touched the bow, it was broken into several pieces. There was a great thunder at the break of the bow. This sound went through all the fourteen worlds. All the creatures of the universe were wonder-struck to hear such a heavy sound. The chariot of the sun stopped. The elephants of the ten directions began to cry due to the thundering sound of the bow. In this way this thundering sound was an information for all the worldly creatures of the universe that, the bow of Lord Shiva has been broken by Lord Sri Ram. Hearing this sound Rishi Parshuram came there at the place of Swayambar. Rishi Parshuram was a great saint, but he was famous for his anger. When he came there all the kings stood from their seat in his honour. Rishi Vishwamitra also saluted him. Ram and Laxman also touched the feet of Parshuram. He was much pleased to see Ram and Laxman with Rishi Vishwamitra. As he saw the broken bow of Lord Shiva, he became very angry. Being a great saint he was famous for his anger and bravery. So everyone was much worried at the arrival of Rishi Parshuram. He asked in the roaring voice, who has broken this bow of my Lord Shiva? No one could speak even a single word with his fear. In the meanwhile, Laxman stood and bowed low in the feet of Rishi Parshuram. He spoke gently, why are you going so angry at the breaking of an old bow? You are a great saint. You should not become so angry like this. At this the anger of Rishi Parshuram reached at the peak. His face become red and he began to shiver with anger. Laxman requested him not to become so angry, because the bow was so old. He said gently that as Ram touched the bow it was turned into several pieces. So there is no fault of Sri Ram. You ought not be angry like this.

छुवत टूट रघुपति न दोषू, मुनि बिनुकाज करिय कित रोषँ।
Chuwat tut raghupati na doshu, muni binukaj kariya kit ronsh.

With piercing eyes Rishi Parasuram roared at Laxman and asked him to leave the swayambar place. Laxman smiled at this and said, you please close your eyes and assume that I am not standing before you. At this humour of Laxman, Parasuram raised his pharsa on Laxman. Now Ram rose from his seat and forbade Laxman not to speak like this with the elders. Laxman sat down silently. Ram bowed his head in the feet of Rishi Parasuram and requested him to excuse the misbehaviour of Laxman. Hearing the sweet voice and seeing the gently behaviour of Ram, Rishi Parasuram was much influenced. His temper went low. He recognised Lord Ram. Parasuram bowed low and saluted many times in the feet of Lord Sri Ram. Now king Janak took the sigh of relief. Parasuram prayed their Lord for a while and went away in the forest for penance.

In this way everybody took the sigh of relief. Everyone was much pleased at the bravery of Sri Ram. This news spread in whole Janakpur that Ram the Prince of Ayodhya has broken the bow. King Janak called his daughter Sita the princess at the Swayambar place.

Queen Sunaina the mother of Sita took princess Sita to the Swayambar gently. Sita put the marriage garland in the neck of Sri Ram and Sri Ram also did the same. Thus, the condition of the Swayambar was fulfilled. And Sri Ram married Sita. But Rishi Vishwamitra suggested to king Janak that the breaking of the bow, the marriage of Ram and Sita was done automatically, even then you please perform your family rituals and customs. He also suggested Janak to inform king Dashratha about this good news. King Janak did the same. King Janak sent a letter with honour to Dashratha the king of Ayodhya. He invited king Dashratha to come to Janakpur with a marriage party because prince Ram has fulfilled the condition of Sita Swayambar. In this way Sita has been married with Ram. So we have to pay our formality of marriage ceremony. The ambassador of Janak ran towards Ayodhya. He reached Ayodhya and gave the letter to the king Dashratha.

When king Dashratha came to know this news that our prince Ram has broken the bow in the Swayambar of Sita at Janakpur, He Jumped in his seat with joy. Just then he sent the information to the queens. All the queens and other people of palace were overjoyed to listen this news. When the citizens of Ayodhya came to know about this pleasant news, they gathered at the palace to know more about this good news. King Dashratha gave several things in donation to the brahmans and the poors. He also gave donation to those persons who came there before him at that time. The queens were also giving donation wholeheartedly. Even king Dashratha tried to give some presents to those ambassadors also who had come from Janakpur to give him the information about the marriage of Ram and Sita, but they refused to take it. They went back to Janakpur very pleasantly. They told Janak all about the greatness of Ayodhya and King Dashratha.

On getting the invitation of king Janak, Dashratha consulted with Guru Vashishtha about the marriage. Guru Vashishtha thought minutely. He also consulted books of astrology and stars in concern to the marriage. Thus after a hard task, he declared the date of marriage of the prince Ram. Now king Dashratha informed king Janak about the date of the marriage. Janak started to make preparations for the marriage. He was waiting for the date of the marriage impatiently. The whole of the city was decorated like a bridegroom. Every citizen of Janakpur was fond of to welcome the marriage party of king Dashratha. Several gates of Banana plants were made to welcome their guest. The flags of the mango leaves were decorated at every gate of the city.

On the other hand in Ayodhya, king Dashratha asked Sumantra to prepare a marriage party. Sumantra the Prime Minister of king Dashratha arranged a grand marriage party. On the due date the marriage party started for Janakpur. In the way to Janakpur, Rishi Bharadwaj welcomed them at his ashram. There was a good arrangement of every comfort for the marriage party. Everybody was wonder-struck to see the better arrangement for everyone in the forest. There was Mangal in the Jungle. They enjoyed several dishes as a feast of palace. In the morning the marriage party started towards Janakpur. As they reached Janakpur, king Janak came out of the city to welcome the marriage party. King Janak highly welcomed everyone. Firstly, he touched the feet of Guru Vashishtha. Then he met king Dashratha with great affection. King Janak arranged all types of comfort for the marriage party. Everybody of the party was much pleased and satisfied with the better arrangement of Janak.

On the other day king Janak paid all types of formalities of marriage according to custom and tradition of their family. King Janak married the four sons of Dashratha, Ram, Laxman, Bharat and Shatrughan with his four daughters Sita, Urmila, Mandavi and Shrutikirti in a proper way. Marriage ceremony was fulfilled in a better way by learned pandits. King Janak gave thousands of elephants, horses, cows and other precious things to Dashratha in dowry. He also gave a lot of golden coins, diamonds and pearls to king Dashratha. He donated several precious things to all the members of the marriage party. When king Dashratha saw his sons with their bridegrooms, he was much pleased. He felt a heavenly pleasure at that time. He thanked his life.

मुदित महीपति सकल सुत,
बघुन्ह समेत निहारि।
जनु पायो महिपाल मनि,

कियन्ह सहित फल चारि॥
Mudit mahipati sakal sut,
Baghunah samet nihari.
Janu payo. mahipal mani,
Kiyanh sahit phal chari.

    King Janak with all of their countries, relatives and citizens served all the members of the marriage party wholeheartedly. Different types of dishes were prepared for the members of the marriage party. At the time of supper and dinner, the women of Janakpur sang mangal geet. The mangal song was sung for the welfare of the family. Every citizen of Janakpur was paying great regard to the persons of Ayodhya, who had come in the marriage party. The residents of Ayodhya were also feeling heavenly pleasure in Mithilapuri. The regard, the honour, the love and the service of the family members of King Janak towards the marriage party was praise-worthy. People of Ayodhya forgot about their home. King Dashratha stayed there for a long time in Mithilapuri.

    After some time, one day Rishi Vashishtha and Rishi Vishwamitra made a proposal before king Janak that king Dashratha wants to go to Ayodhya. Please Janak let him go to see his home. In this way king Dashratha come back to Ayodhya with all of his marriage party. He had found a great deal of dowry in Janakpur. In Ayodhya everybody was waiting impatiently for their Ram with all the brothers. All the mothers were ready to welcome their new brides in the palace. As the marriage party reached Ayodhya, several type of side drums, washdrums, clinets, flutes and other music instruments were played with a heavy sound to inform the citizens about the reaching of the marriage party. When the citizens of Ayodhya came to know about the marriage party, they decorated their houses. The roads and streets were also well washed and decorated with mango leaves and banana plants. Flags with the sign of OM were hoisted at every home of Ayodhya. The streets of the market were filled with fine smell. Different type of well decorated jugs were kept before every houses. Seeing the decency and decorum of Ayodhya, the gods and even Brahma also felt suspicion. They were feeling a great pleasure to see the decoration of Ayodhya. The decoration of the palace of King Dashratha was very pleasant.

    All the mothers with the team of women came at the gate of the palace to welcome their princess. They did not care for their body. They donated a lot of good things to the brahmans. They worshipped Ganeshji and Lord Shiva. The mothers were so happy as a poor man gets every thing of their want. Specially these wants are in four in number. they are Dharm, Arth, Kam and Moksha. Every learned person wants to have these four things. There is nothing more in this world beyond these four things.

The mother were so much pleased that they were unable to move in a fast speed towards the gate of the palace. They were willing to see their Ram very soon. They arranged all the necessary things of worship in a golden plate, for worshipping their Ram. The gentle ladies were coming and going at their galleries in wait of their Ram like the lightening comes and goes in the cloud. The clinets and drums were producing sound like the thunder of the clouds. The beggars were chattering in the streets like frogs and peacock in the rainy season.

Seeing the proper time, Guru Vashishtha ordered Ram to enter in Ayodhya city. Remembering Ganeshji, King Dashratha entered in the city with his four sons. All the citizens of Ayodhya were much pleased to see their Ram and other three brothers with their wives. In this way they came at the gateway of the palace. The mothers worshipped their sons with their wives. People were seeing the couple of Ram and Sita again and again and thanking their lives. The gods were showering flowers from the sky, and bowing their hands towards their Lord Ram and Sita. After worshipping and performing the customs and traditions of the family, the mothers took them all in the palace. They were seated on a well decorated throne in the palace. The mothers welcomed the new brides again in the palace. At this time, seeing their sons, the mother were so happy as the blind man becomes happy on getting back his eyes, as the permanent ill man gets nectar, as the saint gets his God before him, as the poor man gets Parasmani, as the brave man gets victory in the war. The mothers were completing their formalities but the couples had a feeling of suspense inside. Seeing the pleasant behaviour and pleasant atmosphere Ram smiled within himself.

Now King Dashratha gave several things to those, who had gone in the marriage party. He donated them vehicles, clothes, jewels and other good things of their need. They went back to their homes after blessing Ram. The beggars found every thing of their want. All the servants of the palace got things of their need, whatever they wanted.

At last king Dashratha with Rishi Vishwamitra and Guru Vashishtha entered in the palace. When the queens saw gathering of the brahmans in the palace, they came forward and touched the feet of brahmans. They worshipped Rishi Vishwamitra with all the Brahmans and touched their feet again and again. They also worshipped the feet of their Guru Vashishtha. They requested them again and again for their kind mercy. Thus, Rishi Vishwamitra, Guru Vashishtha and all the brahamans blessed the king and the queens pleasantly. The king gave great regard to all the relatives and guests. The gods showered the flowers from the sky to see the marriage celebration of their Lord Sri Ram. In this way the gods went to their abode talking to each other about the gentle behaviour of their Lord Sri Ram.

Now king Dashratha entered in the inner portion of the palace. They took the new brides in their lap like their daughter and asked their welfare. Every one of the palace was very much pleased to see happiness of the people. King Dashratha described all before the queens what had happened in Janakpur. He described in detail the gentleness, the richness, the greatness and the virtues of king Janak. King Dashratha described the goodness of king Janak in many ways. The queens were feeling pleasure to hear the description of king Dashratha. King took bath with their sons. He invited the Guru and brahamans on feast. Different type of dishes were prepared for them. They enjoyed the delicious food pleasantly. The women were singing mangal Geet. In this way the night was very pleasant for everyone. After enjoying the food tasteful betel was given to everybody.

Everyone bowed their head before Sri Ram and went away to their homes. In their way people were describing the greatness and gentleness of Sri Ram and saying that even goddess Saraswati, Vedas, Brahma, Shiva and Ganeshji cannot dare to describe the virtue of Sri Ram, then how we can say something about their greatness and gentleness.

When all of the guests went away, king Dashratha called the queens and informed them, that you all have to look after these new brides as your own daughter. Saying this he went away to their bedroom for sleeping. The bedroom of all the princess was preprepared. So they all went to their bedrooms for rest and sleep. When mother Kashilya saw the tender body of Ram, she asked, the way route of the dense forest is very fearful. That is full of dangerous beasts and demons. How you have killed Tarka, Mareech and Subahu. All these were very dangerous and powerful demons. At this Ram replied gently, with the blessing of Guru Vishwamitra, my father and you, and God also has saved us from all worries. We both brothers were looking after yagna mandap of Guru Vishwamitra and by his blessings we achieved all types of education there. Thus, the mothers pacified Ram with gentle words and asked him for sleeping. They woke up early in the morning. They touched the feet of their mothers, father, Guru and brahmans. They became please on getting the blessings. They went to take bath with their father in the pious river Saryu. When they became fresh, king Dashratha called them in the court. All the courtiers became much pleased to see Ram with all four brothers. After some time Rishi Vishwamitra and Vashishtha came there. They were seated on a fine seat. King touched the feet of them with all of his sons. Seeing Ram both of the Guru became very pleased. Guru Vashishtha preached them about the history of religion, the king and the queen listened him very charmly. He also described about the good deeds of Rishi Vishwamitra in detail. This system continued for long time. Thus, Ayodhya became the place of pleasure like heaven.

One day Rishi Vishwamitra asked the king Dashratha to let him go to his ashram, but Ram requested him to stay for some time more. After sometime he again became ready to go to his ashram, the king stood before him with their sons and bowed low in his feet. He said, this is all due to your grace. So please be kind to us. He blessed them all and went away to his ashram. In the way, he was remembering the virtues of Ram, the devotion of king and about the pleasure of marriage pleasantly.

When Ram came back to Ayodhya with all his brothers, Ayodhya became the place of pleasure from them. The marriage ceremony of Lord Sri Ram was so pleasant that nobody could describes its grandness. In this way, Goswami Tulsidas says that I have described the virtues of Lord Sri Ram to make my tongue pious. Because the virtues and greatness of Sri Ram are like ocean. And nobody can dare to cross it. In the same way nobody could describe the virtues of Sri Ram with their tongue. Even then the persons who will sing the song about the marriage of Sita and Lord Sri Ram, they will get permanent pleasure for ever.

सिय रघुवीर विवाहु, जे सप्रेम गावहिं सुनहिं।
तिन्ह कहुँ सदा उछाहु, मंगलायतन राम जसु॥

Siya Raghuvir vivahu, je saprem gavahi sunahi,
tinh kahun sada uchhahu, mangalyatan Ram jasu.

Thus, Sri Ram Charit Manas is the destructor and washer of all the evils of Kaliyug.

Meeting Of Bharat and Ram

बरबस लिए उठाइ उर, लाये कृपा निधान।
भरत राम की मिलनि लखि, बिसरे सबहि अपान॥
Barbas liye uthai ur, laye kripa nidhan.

Bharat Ram ki milani lakhi, bisrey sabahi apaan.
Chapter 2
AYODHYA KAND

First of all Goswami Tulsidas bowed his head in the feet of Lord Shiva, who is honoured by all the gods. He is requesting Lord Shivaji to defend him from all botherations. Then he requests to Lord Sri Ram, who seems very charming with mother Sita, to be merciful on him. After that in the beginning of Ayodhya kand, first of all he remembers his guru to be merciful on him through which he could get sufficient knowledge to describe the virtues and greatness of Lord Sri Ram, which is capable to give four fruits of life. These fruits are Dharam, Arth, Kam and Moksha. It is said and it is our faith also that if anybody begets these four fruits of life, it means his life is successful. It means he has achieved his goal.

The marriage of Ram and Sita is an extra ordinary marriage, because Sita is not only a simple daughter of king Janak, she herself is goddess Laxmi. She is the creator, the mother and destructor of the whole universe. All the creatures have been created by her. That is why goswami Tulsidas says :

जनक सुताजगजननि जानकी, अतिसय प्रिय करूना निधान की।
ताके युग पद कमल मनावउँ , जासु कृपा निरमल मति पावउँ॥

Janak sutajagjanani janaki, atisay priya karuna nidhan ki.
Take yug padh kamal manavaun, jasu krupa nirmal mati pawaun.

When Ram came back to Ayodhya after marrying Sita, people of the whole city were much pleased to see their Ram. There was joy everywhere. All the wealth of the world was present in Ayodhya. It seemed that Brahma, the creator of the whole universe has shown all their virtues to decorate Ayodhya. People of Ayodhya were much pleased by all means and by all sides to see their loving Ram. The mother with their friends were much pleased to see that their wish is fulfilled by God. Even the king Dashratha was also overjoyed to see the gentle nature of Ram. Every citizen of Ayodhya was thinking within himself that by the grace of God Ganeshji, king Dashratha ought to give the throne to his elder son Ram as a king of Ayodhya.

One day king Dashratha was sitting in his court with all of his courtiers. Ram were also present there. King Dashratha saw his face in the mirror. He gave a set to his crown. At that time he saw that his hair is going to be white. It seemed that he is going to be old. So he thought within himself that he should give throne to his elder son Ram according to the custom of the family. Thinking like this, one day king Dashratha went to Guru Vashishtha and reported about his wish in his feet. The king said, our Ram has become virtuous and capable in all respect. Everyone loves Ram like me. All our relatives also think that Ram is worthy as a king. So I wish to arrange for the coronation of Ram. You please suggest me in this matter. Vashishtha became glad to hear the proposal of king Dashratha about the coronation of Ram. He said, listen king, your son Ram is not an ordinary man. He is supreme power the almighty God. And nobody could get relief in this world without the devotion of Ram. Thus, you are lucky one. So, you please go and arrange all the necessary things of coronation. The king at once came back to palace. He called Sumantra the Prime Minister and other courtiers to get concern about the preparation of the coronation. They also said that our Ram is perfect for every walk of life. All types of abilities are present in him. So, he must be throned. all the courtiers became glad to hear this news. They appreciated king Dashratha for this idea. So the king asked them to arrange all the necessities which was needed for coronation. Guru Vashishtha told them all about the things which was described in Vedas and Puranas for the preparation of the coronation. Whatever Rishi asked them, everything was fully arranged. In the palace, when the queens came to know this news, they became very glad. They donated several things, what they found at that time. There was pleasure everywhere in Ayodhya. Many gates of banana plants were made in the city. Every gate of Ayodhya was decorated with mango leaves. Thousands of elephants, horses and chariots were prepared for the celebration.

With the suggestion of king Dashratha, Guru Vashishtha went to Ram to inform him about the coronation. Ram touched the feet of his guru and asked about his duties. Guru Vashishtha told them all about his formal and moral duties. When every citizen of Ayodhya was waiting impatiently for the coronation of their Lord Ram, they were thinking that their Ram with Sita will sit on the golden throne tomorrow, at the same time gods were not satisfied with this preparation. The gods were thinking that if our Lord Sri Ram will become the king of Ayodhya, then who will kill the cruel demons of the earth. They thought that Sri Ram should go to forest for the welfare of worldly creatures, saints, sages, brahmans and cows. So they requested goddess Saraswati to change the brain of king Dashratha and queens.

Goddess Saraswati unwillingly went to Ayodhya. She changed the brain of Manthara, the old female servant of palace. Mantra was the inner servant of Kaykeye. With the effect of goddess Saraswati, the brain of Manthara was completely changed. Now she began to think not for the good coronation. Manthara went to the younger queen Kaykeye and advised her to oppose the coronation. She suggested Kaykeye to ask two blessings from king Dashratha.

दुइ वरदान भूप सन थाती, माँगहु आज जुड़ावहु छाती।
Deyi vardan boop san thathi, mangahu aaj judawahu chhati.

Somehow Kaykeye agreed with Mantra. She made up her mind to change all the happiness into sadness. In this way she changed all her princely dress. She threw it away and wearing the shabby dress she went into dark room (the Kop Bhawan). When king Dashratha came to know about this fact that his beloved queen Kaykeye has gone in to Kop Bhavan, he went there and asked her the reason of this all. He was wonder-struck to see his queen in such a miserable condition. He could not understand the trick of the queen Kaykeye.

जानि न जाइ नारि गति भाई।
jaani na jayi naari gati bhai.

King Dashratha tried to pacify Kaykeye but failed. When king Dashratha asked her again and again about her anger, she told him angrily that once upon a time you promised me to give two blessings. Now I wish that you please fulfil my requirement. Firstly, I want that you to send Ram to the forest for fourteen years inspite of coronation. Secondly, she asked the king to throne Bharat as a king of Ayodhya. King Dashratha was astonished at this. He asked kaykeye not to think like this. He told her that it will not be good for the palace. But Kaykeye did not heed it. She could not change her idea, because she was not in favour of coronation of Ram. She was rigid and firm on her demand. Thus, the result was clear. The whole situation was turned. King Dashratha became undone. He was not able to think what to do what not to do. So, he impatiently called on Sumantra, the Prime Minister of Ayodhya, to present Ram before him very soon. Sumantra thought for a while. He did the same. He went to Ram at once, and told him that king Dashratha wants to see you immediately. Please come with me immeditely. When Ram heard about it, that king has called him urgently, he was much worried. He followed Sumantra at once. Everyone who saw that Ram is going to the king in such hury, was astonished. Ram sat nearby Dashratha and saw the king Dashratha lying on the ground. Ram asked his father about this at all. The king Dashratha could not speak even a single word. In the meantime, Kaykeye spoke. She told Ram all about the fact, what had happened with the king. She asked Ram to go to forest for fourteen years, if he wants to remove the pain of his father. Ram listened all silently. There was no sign of frustration, strain, anger and worriness at the face of Ram. he smiled and spoke gently, well mother, listen! "The son who follows the order of his parents is lucky one in this world."

सनु जननि सोह सुत बड़ भागी, जो पितु मातु वचन अनुरागी।
तनय मातु पितु तोषनहारा, दुर्लभ जननि सकल संसारा॥
धन्य जन्म जगती तल तासू, पितहि प्रमोदु चरित सुनि जासँ।
चारि पदारथ करतल ताके, प्रिय पितु मातु प्रान सम जाके॥

Sanu janani soh sut bad baghi, jo pitu matu vachan anuragi.
Tanya matu pitu toshanhara, durlabh janani sakal sansara.
Dhanya janma jagati tala tasu, pitahi pramodu charit suni jhans.
Chari padarath kartal take, priya pitu matu pran sam jake.

Saying these words Ram went to get the permission from his mother Kaushalya. King Dashratha could speak nothing due to sadness. When the people of Ayodhya came to know this fact, that our lovable Ram is going to the forest inspite of coronation everyone was much bothered. All the happiness of the palace was turned into sadness. Every citizen of Ayodhya was abusing and insulting Kaykeye for her bad deeds. Even then people began to think in opposition of the women generation. They said, "Nothing is impossible for a woman. She could do any thing, either that is suitable or not."

काह न पावक जारिसक, का न समुद्र समाइ।
का न करै अबला प्रबल, केहि जग काल न खाइ॥

Kah na pawak jarisak, ka na samudra samaii.
Ka na karaye abla prabal, kehi jag kal na khaii.

Some women and other queens also went to Kaykeye, and asked her to change her idea about Sri Ram, but she did not heed for them.

Now Ram touched the feet of his mother Kaushilya and asked for permission to go to the forest. She permitted Ram to fulfil the wish of the king and the mother Kaykeye. At the same time when Sita came to know that her husband Lord Sri Ram is going to forest for fourteen years, she also got ready to go with him. Ram forbade her not to go with him in the forest, because the jungle life is so much troublesome. He told Sita about the troubles and pains of the forest. He further told her that there are several types of wild animals in the dense forest. The paths are full of thorns and we have to go their on foot. There are big and deep rivers to cross. In the forest there will be no bed, we have to sleep on the ground. There will be no rich food at all. We have to eat fruits only. The cruel and dangerous man eater demons roam in the forest. The drinking water of the forest is also not good for health. There are countless of hardships in going to the forest. So please mind for my words. You live here in the palace pleasantly and serve my parents.

When Sita found that Sri Ram will not take her with him to the forest, tears appeared in her eyes. She said, "Well my lord, all type of worldly pleasure is worthless for me in your absence." I need nothing. I wish to serve your feet.

प्रान नाथ तुम बिनु जग माहीं, मो कह सुखद कतहु कछु नाहीं।
जिय बिनु देह नदी बिनु बारी, तैसिय नाथ पुरूष बिनु नारी॥
मैं सुकुमारी नाथ बन जोगू, तुमहि उचित तप मो कह भोगँ।

Pran nath tum binu jag mahi, mo kah sukhad katahu kachu nahin
Jiya binu deh nadi binu baari, tesiya nath purush binu naari.
Mein sukumari nath ban jogu, tumahi uchit tap mo kah bhong.

Hearing the tender voice of Sita, Ram was bound to take Sita with him. Sita touched the feet of their parents and took permission to go to forest with her husband.

In the mean time Laxman got this news. He came to Ram and touched his feet with the tears in their eyes. Laxman also requested Ram to take him to the forest with him. He was fond of serving the feet of Ram and Sita in the troubles also. Somehow Sri Ram agreed to take Sita and Laxman with him to the forest for fourteen years, in the meantime the younger queen Kaykeye brought some dress of saints and kept it before Ram. She spoke in a sweet tone, the king loves you dearly, so he will never allow you to go to forest. In this way now you please think of your duty yourself. Thus, Ram, Laxman and Sita dressed in the garment of the saints. They bowed low in the feet of their parents and started on foot towards the forest. Every citizen of Ayodhya was undone to see their Ram going towards the forest. Ram tried to pacify their Guru Vashishtha and other family members to look after their parents. He requested Guru Vashishtha that our Bharat and Shatrughan are very young. So they have to take care of both younger brothers and even kingdom Ayodhya also. He also requested his Guru to look after their subjects as own son.

Thus, he touched the feet of Guru Vashishtha and his mothers and started towards the forest after praying God Ganeshji. Obeying the King Dashratha, Sumantra, the Prime Minister of Ayodhya prepared a beautiful chariot. Sumantra requested Sri Ram to ride on it. There was a great regard about Sumantra in the heart of Sri Ram. So he rode on the chariot with his younger brother Laxman and beloved wife Sita. Bowing their heads to Ayodhya, they moved towards the forest. It was the time when whole of the Ayodhya was weeping. Women, children, old and young people of Ayodhya followed them to the forest. Somehow people came back to their homes from the forest. Now the chariot of Ram reached Shringberpur. Ram, Laxman and Sita with Sumantra saluted the pious river Ganga. They took bath in the pious river of Ganga and drank its cold water to quench their thirst. They stayed there for the night.

When Kewat the Nishad Raj came to know that Lord Sri Ram has stopped on the bank of the pious river Ganga, he asked his brothers happily. Kewat took some fresh fruits and flowers as presentation and kept it before Lord Sri Ram. He looked at the Lord with love. Kewat put those fruits in the leaf pots before them. Sumantra with Ram, Laxman and Sita ate those fruits and drank water. Now kewat arranged at once some grass made mats. He also prepared a hut at the bank of Ganga with the help of his family members. He asked Ram to take a little rest there. In the night Ram and Sita slept and Laxman began to guard them with the bow in his hands in a scort posture. In the mean time Kewat came there and sat by the side of Laxman. He looked at the shining face of Lord Sri Ram and thought within himself, "The base of the world, the creator of the world, Jagat Pita is sleeping in the necked ground. This is the wonderful system of Brahman. He became very sad and used some insulting words for Kaykeye. Laxman forbade Kewat not to think like this. He gave some spiritual preaching to Kewat at that time. Laxman said, "nobody is responsible for the pain and pleasure of anybody. Please look, hear and argue within yourself and you will find that, pleasure pain, heaven and hell, wealth and poverty all is due to affection for worldly things." He further said to Kewat, that please leave these thoughts aside and come in the feet of Lord Sri Ram by all sides with body, mind and soul. Ram is beyond our thinking. The fact is this that even our four Vedas could not describe the actions and creations of Lord Sri Ram. So, Ram is untouched from worldly pain and pleasure. Thus, Laxman said to kewat, "My friend, leave such thoughts aside and surrender yourself in the feet of Sita and Ram. Sita is Jagat Janani and Ram is Jagat Pita."

In this way the night passed. It became morning. The sun rose and the birds began to chatter in their nests, Sita and Ram awoked. After becoming fresh they asked kewat to bring some milk of Banyan tree. Kewat did the same. Ram and Laxman settled their hair with the milk of Banyan tree. Sumantra saw all these things and began to weep bitterly. He tried once again to take Ram back to Ayodhya in the words of King Dashratha, but Ram was firm like a rock on their determination. Now Sumantra requested Sita to go back with him to Ayodhya as the base of the life of King Dashratha. But she also refused politely and said:

आरत बस सनमुख भयउँ, बिलगु न मानव तात।
आरज सुत पद कमल बिनु, बादि जहाँ लगि नात॥

Aarat bas sanmukh bhayaun, bilagu na manav tat.
Aaraj soot pad kamal binu, badi jahan lagi nath.

Now Sumantra turned their chariot towards Ayodhya bowing his head in the feet of Ram and Sita. At this time he was all alone in the chariot. This is the effect of love about their Lord that the houses of the chariot were not ready to go to Ayodhya leaving there Ram and Sita. Not only men but the animals were also loving their Ram by heart. Somehow, Sumantra reached Ayodhya with the blank chariot. On the other hand Ram with Laxman and Sita went on the bank of the pious river Ganga. Ram asked Kewat to bring the boat for crossing the river. Kewat said, "Well Lord, I know the magic power of your feet. So without washing your feet I may not allow you to sit on my boat. I have heard that with a little touch of your feet, a stone has turned into a shape of beautiful lady. And my boat is made of wood. Thus, it will very easily turn into shape of a lady with the touch of your feet, because the wood is very tender in comparison to the stone. Then what shall I do, this boat is the only base to feed my family. I belong to a very poor family. Somehow, I am feeding my one wife. When there will be two wives, what shall I do then? How shall I feed them? The whole of my family will die of hunger. Kewat further said:

चरन कमल रज कहँ सब कहहीं, मानुष करन मूरि कछु अहहीं।
छुवत सिला भइ नारि सुहाई, पाहन ते न काठ कठिनाई॥
यहि प्रति पालहु परिवारू, नहि जानउँ कछु और खभारू।
जौ प्रभु पार अवसि गा चहहूँ, मोहिं पद पदुम परवारन कहहूँ।
केवट राम रजायसु पावा, पानि कठौता भरि लै आवा।
अति आनन्द उमगि अनुरागा, चरन सरोज पखारन लागा॥

Charan kamal raj kahn sab kahehin, Manush karan moori kachu Ahahin.
Chuvat sila bai naari suhayi, phan te na kath katinayi.
Yahi prati palahu parivaru, nahi janaun kachu aur khabaru.
Jaou prabhu par avasi ga chahahun, mohin pad padum parvaran kahahun.
Kewat Ram rajayasu pawa, pani kathota bari laye aawa.
Ati anand umagi anuraga, charan saroj pakharan laga.

So this is my final decision that without washing your feet, I would not take you across the Ganga river. If you really want to cross it, please let me wash your feet. Ram smiled and looked towards Sita, because she was the only owner of those feet. Sita could not speak anything. Ram understood the sense of Sita and permitted Kewat to wash his feet. He said I have to cross the river just now. Please do not be late. On getting the permission of Ram, Kewat brought water in a big wooden pot. He began to wash the lotus like feet of Lord Sri Ram. At this time gods were showering flowers from the sky on Sri Ram. They praised the fate of Kewat and said that Kewat is very lucky. He washed the feet of Sri Ram and drank it with all of his family members. Thus, he made his way clear to cross the Bhawasagar. How he took Ram, Laxman and Sita across the pious river Ganga. They came down from the boat on the other bank of the river Ganga.

Now Ram thought within himself that I should pay something to Kewat as for charge of the boat but he had nothing to pay for him. He looked towards Sita. Sita, at once, understood the mentality of Sri Ram. Shri Ram tried to give her ring to Kewat as the fare charge of the boat, but he refused to take it. He laid down in the feet of Sri Ram and requested that I have gotten every thing today. Now I need nothing. He further said that when you please come back to Ayodhya from exile, I shall take, whatever you will give me. Thus, Ram departed from Kewat. Sita worshipped the pious river Ganga and asked blessings for the goodness of Ram and Laxman. After taking the blessing from mother Ganga they started towards the forest on foot. On reaching Prayag, Rishi Bharadwaj welcomed Ram. Now Ram, Laxman and Sita took bath in Sangam and they praised the dignity of Sangam in this spiritual world. Rishi Bharadwaj presented some fruits before them Ram with Laxman and Sita ate those fruits pleasantly. When the residents of Prayagraj came to know about the reaching of Sri Ram, at the ashram of Rishi Baharadwaj, they gathered at the ashram to see their Ram. They bowed low before Ram in honour, and Ram also did the same in response. Ram stayed there at night. On the other morning, after taking bath in Sangam, they started their journey. They crossed the pious river Yamuna and reached near the ashram of Maharshi Balmiki. In the way the men, women, boys and girls whoever saw them was wonder-struck. There was a natural attraction at the face of Sri Ram, Laxman and Sita, their charming face was worth seeing. They were walking on foot on the ground, so the earth was praising their fate on touching the lotus coloured feet of Sri Ram with the ground.

Whenever they passed by the side of the villages, people used to come out from their houses. They began to ask them the reason of their travelling on foot in the forest. They wanted to know their address. People wanted to talk with them for a while. The village people are thinking within themselves that they have never seen such a handsome personality in the life. No worldly beauty can be compared with these personalities, because they were extraordinary, charming and attractive. In this way they were passing from village to village and the villagers welcomed them charmly. In the way to the forest Ram is going ahead, Sita is walking in the middle and Laxman is walking behind them. There was a great care of culture and civilization in the mind of Laxman, this was the reason that he was walking scaping the footsteps of Lord Ram and Sita from right to left.

सीय राम पद अंक बराये, लखन चलहि मग दाहिन बायें।
Siye Ram pad ank baraye, Lakhan chalahi mag dahin bayen.

Not only men but the wild animals of the forest were looking at the charming face of Sri Ram and they praised their fate. They saw a calm and quite place in the forest. There were flowers and fruits everywhere. This was the ashram of Maharshi

Balmiki. In the surroundings of the ashram there was natural scene and beauty. When Sri Ram reached in the ashram of Rishi Balmiki, he highly welcomed them. Because he had found the guest according to his wish. Rishi presented some fruits before them. Ram with Laxman and Sita ate them pleasantly. They were much tired through the journey, so Ram asked Rishi Balmiki, I wish to stay here for some time. Please tell me the proper place to make an ashram. Rishi said, "My Lord you are omnipresent and you are asking me about the proper place for your residence." He said, "If you are asking me, then please listen about the place of your residence. You please reside in the heart of that person, who is always busy in your worshipping and who always respects the saints and sages, cows and brahmans, religion and poors. Please you make your residence in that heart also who feels pleasure by feeding others or by feeding those who are hungry. He further requested Ram to reside in that heart also, who bow their heads before God, Guru and Brahman." In this way the Rishi told Sri Ram the proper place for their residence. Rishi Balmiki asked Sri Ram to reside in Chittrakoot for some time. There is a pious river Mandakini. Rishi Atri and other rishies ar residing there. The place is very clam and quite. So, he suggested Ram to make his ashram to live there like a saint. They were living there in the dress of saint and sages.

When the gods came to know this fact that Sri Ram, the almighty God himself is residing in Chittrakoot, they came there and saluted their Lord many times. They worshipped their Lord by heart. They showered flowers on Lord Sri Ram and said that today we are thankful on your reaching here. We have been waiting here for you from a long time. They prayed Ram again and again. They also told Sri Ram about their troubles and pains in detail. Sri Ram promised them to remove their pains. The gods pleasantly went to their residence. After some time when the people of that area came to know that Lord Sri Ram himself is residing in Chittrakoot, they came there to see their Ram. Sri Ram honoured and welcomed them, and the people were much pleased to see the charming and attractive face of Lord Sri Ram. Everyone was praising their fate to see their Ram with them in forest. There was joy and pleasure everywhere.

Since when Sri Ram came in Chittrakoot, all types of goodness, richness and pleasure was presented on the forest by nature. The natural scene of that ashram became very pleasant and attractive. All the trees were covered with flowers and fruits nearby the ashram. The bird and animals were also chattering with pleasure near the ashram. All the rivers were praising the fate of the river Mandakini because Ram, the almighty and omnipresent God had made their hut on its bank. All the mountains were praising the fate of Vindhyachal and Chittrakoot. There was heavenly pleasure at Chittrakoot at that time.

Ram, Laxman and Sita were passing their days in their ashram of Chittrakoot in a pleasant way. It seemed, they had forgotten the pleasure of the palace of Ayodhya. Sita is also living in the ashram. She is serving her husband pleasantly inspite of all the hardships of the forest life. Now the birds and wild animals are the family members of Sita there. The wives of the saints and sages are behaving with Sita like her mother-in-law. They preached her about the duties of a woman like their own daughter. Thus, with the effect of their love, Sita forgot her mothers. She used to serve them as the could.

In this way Ram, Laxman and Sita are passing their time in the forest roaming and saying different type of pious and historical stories, They all were very happy there in the ashram. The eyes of Sri Ram used to become wet whenever he thinks about their parents, friends, brothers and subjects of Ayodhya. Ram was taking care of Laxman and Sita in the same way as the children take great care of their savings. Goswami Tulsidas says that:

राम लखन सिय जोगवहिं कैसे।
पलक विलोचन गोलक जैसे॥

Ram lakhan siya jogvahin kaise
Palak vilochan golak jaise.

When Sumantra came back to Ayodhya, King Dashratha took him in his arms and asked the welfare of Sri Ram, Laxman and Sita with the tears in his eyes. Sumantra told him all about the happenings what had happened in the forest. He tried to pacify the king with sweet words and said that, "O king! You are a great thinker and a learned personality. You are a scort. I think you have always served the saints and sages. You are well known to this fact that, 'Life and death, all type of pleasure and pain, profit and loss, meeting and departure, all these things are natural proceedings. These things happen according to time and fate, in the same way as night comes after day. Thoughtful persons do not mind for all these things. They take it in a common way." Thus, Sumantra told all about Sri Ram. Hearing these words of his minister, king Dashratha could not check himself.

He fell down on the ground and became senseless. King Dashratha remembered his Ram many times. Several doctors came to control the king's disease. But inspite of all the medical aid, king Dashratha left this world forever saying Ram, Ram. All the queens and citizens of Ayodhya wept bitterly. Everybody was abusing kaykeye. They said that Kaykeye had made Ayodhya orphan. There was hue and cry everywhere in Ayodhya. But all was in vain. At that time Guru Vashishtha came there. He tried to convince them.

He told some religious stories in concern to life and death. He pacified everyone. He arranged the dead body of the king in an oil tub from protection point of view because Ram-Laxman were in the forest. Bharat and Shatrughan were also at their maternal father's home. So, guru Vashishtha sent a messenger to take Bharat and Shatrughan from their maternal father's home.

The messenger went to Bharat. He told them that Guru Vashishtha has called them very soon. Bharat was wonder-struck to listen the words of the messenger. He at once got ready with Shatrughan. They reached Ayodhya without being late. When they reached nearby Ayodhya, they found that the environment of Ayodhya was totally changed. There was silence all around. Bharat tried to know its reason, but nobody could speak or answer him about the fact. When Bharat came to know this fact that King Dashratha has left this world forever due to exile of Sri Ram, he becames very sad and faint. He falls down on earth, the condition of Bharat was very poor. He was undone. Bharat, at once, went to the palace. He asked his mother about the death of the king and about the exile of Sri Ram. Kakeye told her son Bharat all with the crocodile's tear in her eyes. Bharat fainted again when he heard that not only Sri Ram but younger brother Laxman and mother Sita have also gone to the forest with him for fourteen years. He called her names. Bharat said angrily you cruel mother, you should have killed me at the time of my birth. You please just go away from my eyes, I do not like to see such a cruel mother like you. In the meanwhile, Bharat went to mother Kaushilya. She embraced Bharat in her arms and wept bitterly. She said, "Well my son Bharat, Ram, Laxman and Sita left all their princely dresses and with the order of king they dressed themselves with the skin of trees and animals. They went away to the forest before my eyes pleasantly without any hesitation." hearing the pity words of Kaushilya, every body began to weep. People sank in the sea of sorrow.

Bharat thought within himself that this all has happened due to me. So I am the only defaulter, I am the only sinner for all these happenings. At the same time Guru Vashishtha came there. He preached everybody in many ways at that time. Guru Vashishtha suggested Bharat not to become so sad and to do their formal duties which were needed at that time. The dead body of king Dashratha was burnt in sandalwoods. Thus, Bharat did all his formalities according to the custom of the family under the guidance of Guru Vashishtha. Guru asked Bharat to sit on the throne of Ayodhya. Mother Kaushilya was also in this favour. they both said to Bharat to rule Ayodhya and to look after the subjects up to Sri Ram's return. Bharat heard them patiently. He thought deeply within himself and came to the conclusion that I am a sinner. Due to my sin, Lord Sri Ram has gone to forest. And on the throne of Ayodhya there should be a religious king. I am not worthy for the throne.

The situation of today is not like that in the age of Bharat. Now a days, people fight for chair among themselves. There is a contrast between both ages. Bharat is refusing for the throne, it is an ideal of that age. People are fighting for the chair and for their right, this is the ideal of present age. So if we want to have peace in the society, we have to follow the ideal of Bharat.

Bharat requested his Guru and Mothers that he wanted to see his Ram once. Bharat said, it is my firm determination that early in the morning I shall move to meet Sri Ram. It is doubtless that I am a great sinner in the eye of Sri Ram. But Sri Ram is very kind hearted for all either for good or for bad. He will not refuse to meet me. He will excuse me for my mistakes very gently. So certainly we should go to meet our Ram without any hesitation. Every citizen of Ayodhya, all the mothers and the persons of the palace were much pleased to listen these words. They were very pleased as the peacock becomes pleased on hearing the sound of thundering clouds. Thus, everyone started toward Chittrakoot by their own means of transport to see Sri Ram. Everybody was on their vehicle but Bharat was going on foot in the forest also. His legs were injured due to going barefooted without practice. Yet Bharat did not ride on the chariot. He continued to go on foot.

When they reached Shringberpur, Nishad Raj welcomed them warmly. He embraced Bharat in his arms. Nishad Raj asked all of his family members to arrange hundreds of boats. Several boats were arranged at once. Thus, Bharat with all his subjects and family members crossed the pious river Ganga very easily.

Everybody was much tired due to long journey. So, they decided to take a little rest. They ate some fruits and drank the cold water of pious river Ganga. Thus, they took a sigh of relief. Early in the morning Bharat requested to show the place where Sri ram slept in the night. Nishad showed the Shinsupa tree under which Sri ram had passed one night. Bharat went there and saluted that place by heart. He took some sand from that place and rubbed it on his forehead. Thus Bharat had presented an ideal of brotherhood before us. His ideal behaviour towards his elder brother is an ideal for our coming generation also. Our present mislead young generation should take lesson from the ideals of Bharat. The character of Bharat is a mile stone for us. In this connection, I want to say that if our young bloods may follow the ideals of Bharat in concern to brotherhood, thousands of problem may be solved very easily. The ideal character of Bharat is shining in the sky like sun.

On the other hand after taking bath in the pious river Ganga Bharat started their journey. Kewat was showing them the way. After travelling day and night they reached Prayagraj. When the saints and sages came to know that Bharat the younger brother of Sri Ram has come to Prayagraj on foot from Ayodhya, they all come there to take the welfare of Bharat. When they understood the reason that Bharat wants to meet their elder brother Sri Ram and this is why he has come here on foot from Ayodhya, they were much impressed with the character of Bharat. They praised Bharat many times. The saints and sages of Prayagraj were praising their own fate also because they had seen the brother like Bharat. They said that this is the result of our good deeds that we got chance to see Lord Sri Ram. And with the grace of Sri Ram we have gotten chance to see Bharat in prayagraj. In this way, everyone was thanking and praising their fate again and again. At this the gods were showering flowers from the sky on them. The gods were also praising the fate of the people of Prayagraj.

Remembering the painful life of Sri Ram, Bharat was much tired, so the saints and sages requested Bharat to take some rest in Prayagraj. They arranged all the kingly comforts in the service of Bharat and their company in the forest by the grace of their penance. Even Bharat was also perturbed and wondered such type of comfortable things in the forest, which he had never seen in his life. On the other day Bharat with all of the company started towards Chittrakoot. Bharat had left all the princely dress aside. He was walking barefooted in the forest. Seeing the condition of Bharat, the clouds were providing shade in the way to give shelter from excessive heat of the sun. The nature was more favourable to Bharat than to Sri Ram in the way.

On the other hand, one day Sri Ram, Laxman and Sita were sitting hear their ashram. They heard the noise of gathering at some distance. In the mean time the forest dwellers reported Ram all the fact about the noise. Ram began to think again and again about the reason of Bharat's arrival in the forest with all of his army. Laxman understood the worriness of Ram's heart. So, he requested Ram to give permission to ruin Bharat with all of his army. Laxman said that even Lord Shiva can not save Bharat today in the battlefield, because Bharat has insulted my Ram. So he will have to suffer for his deeds. Very patiently Ram said to Laxman that the nature of Bharat is very simple and gently. He may not think like this against me. He is very lovable for me. In the mean time, in the guidance, of Kewat Bharat reached near the ashram of Sri Ram where he saw his Ram, sitting at a distance. Bharat laid down on the naked ground in honour and regard. Laxman found that Bharat is saluting Ram in love, he told Ram about the situation. Ram threw his arms. Whoever saw the meeting of Ram and Bharat at this time, was wonder-struck. After meeting Laxman, Bharat went to touch the feet of mother Sita. At that time very patiently Kewat requested Ram that all the mothers, Guru Vashishtha, other servants and a huge army has come with Bharat. When Ram came to know that Guru Vashishtha has come with them, he, at once, went there and touched the feet of his Guru. Vashishtha embraced Ram with love. Ram met all his mothers and pacified them saying we ought not blame anyone for this because this very world depends upon supreme power of the God. Sri Ram said that it was to be done by nature. In the meantime, Sita also came there and met all the mothers pleasantly. Every one blessed her by heart for a long happy life. Sita served all her mothers in the ashram as she could. When the mothers found Sita in such a dress, they were thinking sadly about the life of Sita. They thought that Sita, who was leading a prosperous life in the palace is roaming in the forest on foot.

In the morning, according to Guru Vashishtha, Ram performed all his formal duties of his dead father. After finishing all the traditional performances of the family he took bath in the pious water of Ganga and became pious himself. They all were hungry, so they took some fruits and drarik water. Now Ram asked to his elders about the further programme. Guru

Vashishtha said, it would be better if Ram and Laxman go back to rule Ayodhya and other two brothers Bharat and Shatrughan would go to forest. Hearing this proposal Bharat became very glad. At this Sri Ram said, I am totally ready to follow the guidance of our Guru. The whole gathering was in purplexion. In the meanwhile, Bharat requested Ram to act which is beneficial for the people. Thus, Bharat laid down on the feet of Ram waited for further order to follow. Ram took Bharat in his arms and got him seated by his side. Everyone was worried to see this scene.

At this time the king of gods Indra thought that our programme is going to be dismissed. So he sent "Maya" to change the mentality of the people. She did the same. Now every body was perturbed with the effect of "Maya". Sometimes they thought for their household duties and some time they thought to live with Ram in the forest. Only Sri Ram could know the influence of "Maya". He smiled at this. Now Ram said to Bharat, you rule and protect Ayodhya until he comes back from the forest. Bharat touched the feet of Ram and request to give him his sandal as the base to pass the schedule time. Ram took him in his arms and blessed him for a long life. Everyone saluted to each other with tears in their eyes. All the forest-dwellers also went away praising the sweet and kind behaviour of Bharat and Ram. Now Ram with Laxman and Sita are sitting in the ashram. People of Ayodhya reached their destination safely. Bharat made his hut in nandi village out side Ayodhya. He began to live there like a saint. He left all his princely dresses and pleasure of life. Everyday Bharat used to worship the sandal of Ram and by its order he began to rule over Ayodhya. Ram and Laxman were residing in the forest and Bharat was passing his days at the same pattern of Ram like a saint. So people used to say that Bharat is praiseworthy by all sides. By his behaviour, Bharat had kept an example of brotherhood before coming generation. In this way, Goswami Tulsidas says that the persons who remember the character of Bharat they may get relief from the pain of Bhawasagar.

भरत महा महिमा जल रासी, मुनि मति ठाढ़ि तीर अबला सी।
तेहि पुर बसत भरत बिनु रागा, चंचरीक जिमि चम्पक बागा॥

Bharat maha mahima jal rasi, muni mati thathi tir abla si
Tehi pur basat bharat binu raga, chancharik jimi champak baga.

Sutikchhan is in the Meditation of Sri Ram

Chapter 3
ARANYA KAND

Lord Shiva says to Parvatiji that the persons who always remember the good deeds of Sri Ram, they get Moksha from the worldly things. And those who have no faith in the feet of Sri Ram they get a lot of worldly pain. Now please listen about the pious character and activities of Lord Sri Ram, which are pleasant to the minds of everyone. Once Sri Ram plucked some flowers and made a garland of it. He decorated it in the hair of Sitaji. They sat on a fine stone in front of the ashram. The son of Indra, Jayant, came there in disguise of a crow. He wanted to know the real power of Sri Ram. He was an evil fellow. So, he made the form of a crow. Now the crow pinched in the feet of Sita with its beak. Blood began to flow from her feet. When Sri Ram saw his misbehaviour, he shot an arrow on him. Due to fear, it flew away. He went to his father Indra the king of gods, but he could not save him. He also went to Brahma and Lord Shiva for shelter but they refused to save him. Goswami Tulsidas who was well known about the supreme power of Lord Sri Ram, he very minutely reminds and says that no one can dare to save him who thinks against Lord Sri Ram. And thus, he was kicked from every where, wherever he went. Rishi Narad saw Jayant in trouble. Having a saint heart, he felt pity on it. Now he suggested Jayant to go in the feet of Lord Sri Ram and say that only Sri Ram may be capable to save his life. Thus, Jayant surrendered himself in the feet of Sri Ram and somehow he was saved. This is the greatness of Marayada Purushottam Lord Sri Ram that he excused their enemy also.

In this way, Sri Ram stayed in chittrakoot for some time among the Rishies and Munies. He preached them about Vedant there. After some time they departed from there towards ahead in the forest. They reached in the ashram of Attri Muni. He welcomed them warmly with all of their followers. He prayed them by heart. Sitaji touched the feet of Anusuiya the wife of Rishi Attri. she blessed Sita for a happy Life. Anusuiya told her all the formal duties of an Indian woman. She told her in detail about the variety of the women. She further told that a woman can get a highter place in the society, if she flowers in the footsteps of her husband. She stressed that the woman was the key point for the development of the society. Now they touched the feet of the Rishi and marched ahead in the forest. In the way, wherever they go, the clouds were giving shade to them, on the way the demon Biradh wanted to eat them but Sri Ram killed him with a little effort. Thus, he came in his original form and found Moksha, after that Rishi Sarbhanga met him in the way. He bowed low and lay down in the feet of Sri Ram. He sat in meditation putting the image of Lord Sri Ram in his heart, and he burnt his body by the help of Yoga fire and went to heaven. Everybody praised the fate of the Rishi Sarbhanga. The rishies prayed them and Sri Ram with Laxman and Sita started forward. On the way, when Sri Ram saw the heap of the bones, he asked them about the fact. They told them the whole history that these were the bones of Rishies and Munies. The demon had eaten them. Hearing this, tears appeared in the eyes of Sri Ram. His heart filled with pity. He thought for a while. He raised his hands and took oath to abolish the demons from the earth.

निशिचर हीन करहुं महि, भुज उठाइ प्रन कीन।
Nishchir heen karahu mahi, bhuj uthaye pran keen.

A disciple of Rishi August named Sutikchhan, who was the devotee of Sri Ram by body, mind and soul came there and prayed him whole-heatedly. Blessing him, Ram moved ahead towards Rishi Kumbhaj from the ashram of August Muni. The followers of Kumbhaj Rishi informed him about the arrival of Lord Sri Ram. In the ashram, Rishi welcomed him warmly and took him in his arms. Rishi worshipped Sri Ram with all of the saints who were present there. Ram Sat among them. Everybody was pleased to see Lord Ram. Now Sri Ram asked the Rishi that you were well known about my arrival in forest. So you please tell me the way through which I may kill the demons who are the enemies of saints and sages. Rishi smiled and said, you are omnipresent. You are almighty. You know all. Nothing is hidden from you. So how I can tell you the way. It is your realness that you are asking the way from me. He pointed towards the Panchvati in Dandak Van and requested him to reside there for some time. Ram went to Panchavati. There he met Vulture King Jatayu. He made him friend. Thus, Sri Ram made his hut on the bank of the river Godavari. When Sri Ram began to live there all types of natural wealth came there by the mercy of Sri Ram. The birds, the animals were also very pleased near ashram. Several types of flowers were showing their beauty.

One day Laxman asked Sri Ram that you are Lord of all. I know it well. But I am asking you like a human being. Please tell me the distinction between God and soul lives that is Ishwar and Jeeva. Please also tell me what is Maya and what is knowledge? Because by knowing this distinction I may be capable to worship more and more in your feet. Sri Ram said, well Laxman! I shall tell you in brief all about your questions. I am very much pleased with your question because it is more beneficial and useful for mankind. Please listen minutely. It is mine and it is your this is Maya. It is mine and it is you, this is also Maya. And this Maya has controlled the whole universe and the whole generation. Whatever you see and think all that is Maya. The whole universe is covered with the influence of Maya. The creature who leaves Maya aside and worships God whole heatedly he may be capable to get his mercy. The person who lives in this mortal world but worldly things cannot influence him, he is my true devotee and I love him most. So, I reside in that heart who remembers me by body, mind and soul. Hearing the words of Sri Ram about the way to Moksha, Laxman bowed his head in the feet of Lord Ram and became very pleased. This preaching was not only for Laxman but for the welfare of the whole worldly creatures.

One day Surpnakha the sister of Demon king Ravan came nearby the ashram. When she saw two handsome princes there, she thought in herself to marry them. This is the natural weakness of a lady that she looks a handsome man with evil eyes either he is her brother or father, son or some one else.

भ्रात पिता पुत्र उरगारी, पुरूष मनोहर निरखत नारी॥
Bhrat pita putra urgari, prush manohar nirkhat naari.

So, she could not check herself. She went to Ram in disguise of very pretty lady and said in smiling mood: "There is no handsome man like you and no beautiful lady like me, in this world, this is the matter of chance. I have been remained unmarried for you." So with the influence of the natural attraction she fell in love to Sri Ram. In this way to fulfil their wish she made a proposal of marriage with Sri Ram. Ram said, I am premarried, you may go to Laxman, my younger brother and indicated towards him. She went to Laxman and made the same proposal. Laxman said to her, listen please I am devotee of Sri Ram. He is the king of Ayodhya. You please go to him. I am undone in this matter. She went to Ram but Sri Ram sent her again to Laxman. Now Laxman insulted her badly for her evil thoughts. So she turned into anger. She came in her original shape. When she attacked on Sita, Laxman cut her ears and nose by sword and in this way he challenged Ravan for war. Without nose and ears her face became very fearful and aweful. In the same position, she went to Khar and Dushan who were the commander in chief of Ravan and told him all, what had happened with her. Khar and Dushan took a huge army of fourteen thousand demons and attacked on Ram. When they reached face to face and saw the handsome personality of Sri Ram, he thought that this is some extraordinary personality. Due to this they could not shoot their arrows on Ram. Thus, they tried Sri Ram to leave the battlefield with his wife. Sri Ram smiled this foolish words and asked them not to talk kindly but to fight. In this way, a fierce battle took place. Within a short time Sri Ram killed all the demons with a little effort.

When Sri Ram won the battle, all the gods, saints and sages became pleased and they also became fearless. Now Laxman came there with Sita and they touched the feet of Sri Ram. Now Sri Ram began to live in Panchvati happily. Their deeds behaviour and their preaching were pleasant for the rishies and munies. When Surpnakha, the sister of demon king Ravan, heard about the defeat of Khar and Dushan, she shivered with fear and she went to Ravan for shelter. She told Ravan angrily that here you are eating and drinking merrily you are sleeping day and night carelessly you don't mind for your kingdom and subjects. She wept bitterly in between the courtiers and said, Ravan, you are alive and I have been insulted in such a way. Your life is worthless. She was seated by a courtier. Ravan asked her that who had cut her nose and ears, my sister. Surpanakha said that the two sons of Dashratha the king of Ayodhya have come in the forest. They are brave like lions. It seems, they will ruin the demon generation from earth, because on behalf of them the saints and sages are roaming in the forest fearlessly. I think in bravery there is no rival of those brothers. They have also a beautiful lady. The lady is peerless in this world. His younger brother has cut my ears and nose. When I called Khar and Dushan for help, he killed them with all of his army. Their bravery is praiseworthy.

When Ravan, the demon ling of Lanka, heard that Khar and Dushan were killed in the battlefield by a prince of Ayodhya, he trembled with anger and fear both. He pacified his sister Surpnakha and went to his palace. But he could not sleep the whole night in concern to this matter. He thought that gods, men and other creatures of the world have no courage to face my commanders, Khar and Dushan, because they were brave like me. If God, the almighty, has incarnated himself to abolish the demon from the earth and to please the saints, then I shall challenge him and make him my enemy. In this way, I shall achieve my goal Moksha. It is my firm determination that I may not worship God in this physical feature. And if they are ordinary sons of any king, I shall kill them in the battle and I will kidnap the beautiful lady from them. In this way, I will kill two birds with one stone. He went alone to his maternal uncle Mareech.

Lord Shiva says to Parvatiji: Listen Parvati the secret of history of Ram. Ram made a plan. When his younger brother Laxman went to the forest for taking the flowers and fruits, Sri Ram smiled and said to Sita that almighty and omnipresent shall do some human like behaviour. So you please reside in fire for some time until I abolish the demons from the earth. When Sri Ram told her all about his deeds, for which he has taken birth on his earth, Sita understood the secret. She touched the feet of Sri Ram and entered and sunk into the fire. She presented herself in the duplicate form but in the same physical feature. Nobody could know the reason of this change. Even Laxman who lived like a shadow with Sri Ram, could not know this secret service what Sri Ram had done. In Sri Ram Charit Manas, there are several occasions, there are several happenings which are total secret. No one can be capable to understand the themes of this secret. Even saints and sages, rishies and munies who were remain worshipping throughout their whole life in the feet of Sri Ram they also could not understand the secret action of Sri Ram.

जो कुछ चरित रचा भगवाना, उमा मरम काहू नहि जाना।
Jo kuch charit racha baghwana, Uma maram kahu nahi Jana.

Thus, Ravan, the demon king of Lanka, who never bowed his head to anyone, he went to Mareech, bowed his head low and saluted in his feet. Here, Goswamiji has very very minutely observed about the natural deeds of evil doors. Through Sri Ram Charit Manas he teaches us that when such type of people who are of evil thoughts talk in a sweet tone, it means they have to do some dangerous work. Their such type of works or behaviour will be painful to the mankind. So, Mareech was much worried to see Ravan there alone with him. Thinking him to be the king of their generation, he welcomed Ravan warmly and asked the reason of his coming alone. Ravan told all the story proudly to Mareech. Ravan asked him to became a golden deer by which he may steal Sita easily. Mareech said to Ravan that he is not an ordinary personality. He is almighty God in the human form. He is the Lord of the whole creatures. He is the creator and destructor both of the whole universe. So, you please never try to make him enemy. He further told Ravan about the power of these princes that when they were guarding the yagna of rishies and munies. He shot without pointed arrow to me and that took me across the sea. Even today also, whenever I remember him I tremble with fear. And if they are human being even then they are very brave. You have no power to oppose them anymore.

लेते ही उनका नाम सखे, जूडी सी चढ़ती आती है।
वह चोट पुराने वर्षों की, फिर आज उभरती आती है॥
Late hi unka naam sakhe, judi si chadti aati hey.
Vah chot purane varshon ki, phir aaj ubharti aati hey.

Mareech says that they have killed the braves like Tarka, Subahu, they broke the bow of Lord Shiva in the Swayambar of Sita, they also killed Khar and Dushan and Trishra who were brave like you, so how you can say that they are ordinary men. Please think twice or thrice for the welfare of your family members and go back to your home silently. Never try to ruin your family. Hearing the advice of Mareech, Ravan became very angry at him. He called him names and said, you are a stupid fellow, preaching me like my Guru. You do not know that there is no rival of mine in the world. Then Mareech thought within himself that the last period of Ravan has come and this is the reason of his behaviour. He thought and came to the conclusion that there are nine things in the world which are not oppose worthy. Their opposition may be dangerous for anyone. They are the person having with arms, the genius, the devotee of God, the doctor, the praiser and the poet etc. If anyone opposes to these nine personalities, he will have to suffer.

नवहि विरोघ नहि कल्याना।
Navahi viroghe nahi kalyana.

Thus, when he saw that death is but certain from both sides, then he remembered the feet of Ram. He thought that if I will not follow this rude fellow, he will kill me undoubtedly. So I should die from the arrow of Sri Ram, because that would be better in many ways for me.

उभय भांति देखेसि निज मरना, तब ताकेसि रघुनायक सरना।

Ubhay bhanti dekhesi nij marna, tab taakesi Raghunayak sarna.

When they reached near that very forest where Sri Ram had made their ashram, Mareech became golden deer. The deer was so attractive and charming and due to this when it was grazing nearby the ashram of Sri Ram, Sita saw the unnatural golden deer, she could not check herself. She requested Sri Ram to kill that very deer and bring the charming skin of it. Here Goswami Tulsidas very minutely observes and says that to take birth of a golden deer is total impossible, yet being almighty Lord Sri Ram also was attracted towards it. It is said that at the time of misfortune, the learned persons also loose their thinking power.

असम्भवं हेम मृगस्य जन्म,
तथापि रामं लुलुभो मृगायः।
प्रायः समापन्नि विपत्ति काले,
धियोऽपिपुसां मलिनी भवन्ति॥

Asambhavam hem mraghasya janma,
Tathapi ramam lulubho Mrighayah.
Prayah samapanni vipatti kale,
dhiyopipusam malini bhavanti.

Though Sri Ram knew it well that what was to happen, when he will follow the deer leaving Sita alone in the dense forest, yet he raised his bow to fulfil the aim of gods. Sri Ram told Laxman that he was going to hunt that deer and he has to take care of Sita very attentively. Be aware from the demons which are wondering here and there in the forest. Seeing Sri Ram the deer ran away in the forest. Taking his bow and arrow, Sri Ram also followed him. This was the matter of wonder that Vedas and Nigamas could not reach upto the feet of that supreme power, even Lord Shiva could not see him in meditation and that Ram was following the Maya Mrig, the golden deer. In the meantime, Sri Ram shot an arrow it pinched in his body and it fell down saying Ram! Ram! loudly. At the time of his death he came in his original physical feature. Now he remembered his Lord Sri Ram by heart. So seeing the inner love of their devotee Ram went to the deer. He gave him Moksha and sent it heaven which is beyond the reach of rishies and munies. Thus, the gods were showering flowers from the sky upon Lord Sri Ram and say that how kind you are? You have send the demon to the heaven. This is only your kindness and nothing else. In Sri Ram Charit Manas, Goswami Tulsidas describes the special quality of Lord Sri Ram which is praised by all. Even his enemies praise him. When Sita was all alone there in the ashram, on getting time Ravan the demon king of Lanka came there in disguise of a saint. He worshipped in the feet of mother Sita by heart and felt a great pleasure within himself. Ravan was wise enough. He knew it well that this Sita is not an ordinary woman. Sita is the mother of the whole world. Inspite of all these, he took her in his chariot towards Lanka.

Sita was all alone there in the forest. She could do nothing. Sita wept bitterly but he did not mind for this. On the way to Lanka, the vulture King jatayu tried to save Sita from Ravan but failed, because he had cut his feathers from his sword. When his feathers were cut down he fell down on the ground saying Ram! Ram! Ravan again took Sita on his chariot and moved forward hurriedly with fear. Sita was weeping in the chariot like a deer in the grip of the hunter. When she saw some monkies sitting on the hills, she dropped her towel from the chariot. In this way, he took Sita to Lanka. Sita refused to live in the palace, so he kept her in Ashok Vatika. Now she was all alone in Ashok Vatika. But she remembered the same form of Lord Sri Ram in which he had followed the unnatural golden deer.

On the other hand when Ram came back to his ashram near Godawari River, he found that Sita was not there. When he came to know the fact that Sita is actually not there he thought that some one has stolen her. So he began to cry and weep. He became very sad like a poor creature. He praised virtues of Sita many times. He started in search out Sita. In the dense forest he asks the trees, birds, animals and insects that whether they have seen Sita anywhere? He is weeping and searching for Sita like a common man of the mortal world. The omnipresent Ram who is the collection of pleasure and who is immortal behaves like a human being in this mortal world.

विरही इव प्रभु करत विषादा।
Virahi iva prabhu karat vishada.

On the way he saw Jatayu lying on the ground. He was saying only Ram! Ram! It seemed that these were the last moments of his life. He was only waiting for Lord Ram to convey him the message of Sita. Sri Ram came to him. As he touched his head with his hands, his whole pain went away. He told all about Sita to Sri Ram. He told that Ravan the demon king of Lanka has taken away Sita with him towards Lanka on his chariot. As Jatayu was about to depart from this world, Sri Ram asked him that if he wants to live more in this world he may be blessed for it. But Jatayu smiled and said, our Vedas and Upanishads says that even a sinner also, if he remembers Sri Ram on his dying time, he begets Moksha. This is the matter of good luck that Lord Sri Ram is present before me. And so there is no need at all to live in this world anymore. Tears appeared in the eyes of Sri Ram and they said well Jatayu, you have achieved the higher place by your good deeds. Now you please leave this and go to heaven. But mind, please you ought not tell any thing concern to kidnapping of Sita by Ravan to my honourable father Dashratha in heaven. I promise you that if actually I am Ram, then very soon Ravan will tell him all these with all of his family. Jatayu left this mortal world and went to heaven worshipping Ram! Ram! It was his good luck that Sri Ram himself made his funeral by their own hands. It is the kind of nature of Lord Sri Ram which gave Jatayu the same place, which the saints and sages achieve after a hard penance.

Lord Shiva says to Parvatiji that listen Uma, those persons are of bad luck, who enjoy the worldly things, inspite of devotion and meditation. Now Sri Ram with Laxman started forward in search of Sita in the forest. When they were passing through the forest a dangerous demon named Kabandha came there. As he was about to attack them, Shri Ram killed him in a stroke. When he fell down dead on the earth, he told them about the curse of Rishi Dubasha. Actually the demon Kabandha was a Gandharva. But due to curse of Rishi Durbasha, he became demon. Thus, with the touch of Sri Ram he again came in his original physical feature. Ram said to Gandharva I never like the opponent of Brahman generation. He further said that the person who serves the Brahman whole heartedly, all the gods with me could be won by him. In this way Ram blessed him and stepped in the ashram of Shabari the Bhilani. When Shabri knew that Lord Sri Ram have come in her ashram, she ran forward and layed down in the feet of Sri Ram. On actually speaking, it was known that shabari was waiting for her Ram from thousand of years. She felt inner pleasure of love and the result was this that she could not speak even a single word from her mouth. Only she bowed her head in the feet of Sri Ram. She fetched cold water and washed the feet of Ram and Laxman. She be seated them on a beautiful white stone in the ashram. She presented some fruits of plums before them to eat and praise its sweetness again and again. Though Shabari was belonging to the backward caste, but being a devotee, she became lovable to Lord Sri Ram. Sri Ram gave her Nawdha Bhakti, the best Bhakti of the world. This is the matter of consideration that if Shabari could go in the feet of Sri Ram and could get Moksha, then why we may not get it. So never forget Him. And He will never forget you. But we have to remember Him by heart and not by tongue only, because the almighty Sri Ram is present in every particle of the world. So the fact is this that no one can cheat Him. He sees everything. He sees all. In this way if we surrender our self in the feet of Lord Sri Ram by all means, certainly He will accept your devotion. And then you may be able to get the kind blessings of Sri Ram like gentle rain soothes the man from chilling sun.

Sri Ram with Laxman left that forest and marched ahead in search of his beloved wife Sita. There was a natural beauty in the forest. It was due to the grace of Sri Ram, but he looked the beauty of the forest like a common man. They were much tired on roaming in the forest and so they become fresh in a tank. Ram with Laxman sat under the shade of a tree. All the gods came there to him. They prayed their God, their Lord Sri Ram again and again and went to their places. Ram and Laxman were pleasantly talking on some religious matters. They were talking on religious ground.

In the meanwhile, when Rishi Narad saw that God himself is suffering from the pain, he thought within himself, that accepting my curse, Sri Ram is suffering from these worldly pains. Rishi Narad went to Sri Ram. He bowed low in the feet of Sri Ram. Ram took him in his arms and be seated him by his side. When Narad saw that Lord Sri Ram is in a good mood he asked, well Ram,, why you have not get me married when I was wiling to marry myself. Ram said very politely, I always take care of my devotees. I guard them in the same way as the mother guards her children.

करहु सदा तिनकर रखवारी।
जिमि बालक राखे महतारी॥
Karahu sada tinkar rakhvari
Jimi balak rakhe mahtari

And in this world women is more dangerous than the other worldly weapons. This fellow is more harmful than anything of the world. Well Narad listen to me what I say. And not only I say but our Vedas and Purans also say that the women ruins all the penance of the man in the same way as summer season sucks or dries the whole water of rainy season. This was the base of all kinds of bad luck, misfortunes and pains, so I had scaped you from all these troubles. Thus, I did not let you marry at that time.

This is the game of fate that I am suffering from the same trouble through which I had saved you. The heart of Narad filled with gratitude. The brain of Naradji was washed naturally. So he requested prabhu Sri Ram to tell the goodness and symptoms of saint and sages. Sri Ram told him that I love only those who are fearless, beyond the pain and pleasure, truthful, poor who have no interest in sexual things who are self satisfied, who are full of virtues, who do not mind for their good health or bad health and who come in my feet leaving all the worldly things aside. Thus, I give him more and more regard than to others.

In this way praying the good deeds of Lord Sri Ram Narad went to Brahmapur. Goswami Tulsidas says on behalf of his own experience that those persons are actually thankful and praiseworthy who have left the attraction and affection of all the worldly pleasure and have surrendered in the feet of Lord Sri Ram. Goswamiji further says that mind is the key point to govern the whole body. And so the mind should not behave like an insect who plays with the flame of the lamp and burns himself. In the same way the body of a lady is like the flame of the lamp. And our mind should always try to escape from the flame, otherwise, it will burn and ruin. There is only one means to escape from this maya which is Satsang. That is to discuss with each other about the God and Godly creations. Talking, reasoning, discussing and arguing are the only means of wisdom. So, to know something about God, it is must to sit with the saints and sages. Only they can guide us to reach or to know the God.

Friendship of Lord Sri Ram with Sugreeva

Sri Ram pacified Sugreeva and said, "Well Sugreeva! I will leave no stone unturned. I will do my best for your welfare."

सखा सोच त्यागहु बलमोरे।
सब विधि घटब काज मैं तोरे॥
Sakha soch tyagahu balmore
Sab vidhi ghatab kaj mein tore.

Chapter 4
KISHKINDHA KAND

Goswami Tulsidas knew it well that Lord Sri Ram is the greatest devotee of Lord Shiva. So firstly, he is praying that Lord Shiva who drank the poison for the welfare of the gods as well as universe singing the song in the praise of Lord Shiva. Tulsidas is bowing his head in his feet and says no God is so kind hearted like Lord Shiva. Lord Shiva is pleased with a little devotion but this devotion should be beyond selfishness.

Now the story of Lord Sri Ram runs forward. Searching for Sita, Sri Ram and Laxman reached near Rishya Mook mountain. There lived Sugreeva the younger brother of Bali with his courtiers. It is said that Bali had kidnapped his wife and beaten him badly. He had also taken all his wealth and other property. So due to fear, Sugreeva had started living in this mountain. Due to curse of a Rishi, Bali could not come on this hill. When Sugreeva saw the two young brave men coming towards him, he feared. And he sent Hanuman to know that who were they? Hanuman went to Ram in the form of a Brahman and asked their address. Hanuman said, it seems, you are not any ordinary personality. The glow of your face and your physique indicate that you have some godly power. So, please tell me your address and how you have come here?

को तुम श्यामल गौर शरीरा, क्षत्रिय रूप फिरहँ वन वीरा।
कठिन भूमि कोमल पद गामी, कवन हेतु वन विचरहुं स्वामी॥

Ko tum shyamal gaur sharira, kshatriya roop phirahn van vira.
Kathin bhumi komal pad gami, kavan hetu van vicharahu swami.

Sri Ram replied we are the sons of king Dashratha, who ruled over Ayodhya. My name is Ram and he is my younger brother Laxman. My wife Sita was also with me. But, here, in the forest some demon has stolen her. So we are wandering here in search of Vaidehi. Well Brahmanji! I have told you my address and now you please tell me your own address. Why you have come to me in the form of Brahman? Now Hanuman recognised his Lord and laid down in the feet of Sri Ram.

प्रभु पहिचानि परेउ गहि चरना, सो सुख उमा जाइ नहिं बरना।
Prabhu pahchani pareu gahi charna, So sukh Uma jaye nahi barna.

Hanuman was overjoyed and so he worshipped his Lord again and again. Then Hanuman took them to Sugreeva on the hills of the mountain Rishya Mook. He took Ram and Laxman on his shoulders and reached Sugreeva. Hanuman made them friends. Both took oath before the fire to help each other. When they became friend, Laxman told them all about Sita. With the tears in the eyes Sugreeva said that, you will get Sita, undoubtedly. He told that once I was sitting here on the hills with all of our courtiers, we saw that by the airways she passed through over our heads. She was helpless and was weeping bitterly. But she saw us, so she had dropped her cloth before me. Ram asked for that cloth. He presented that cloth before Ram. At once Sri Ram recognised the cloth of Sita and became very sad. Then Sugreeva pacified Ram and Sita, that very soon we will do our best to search out Sita. His eyes became wet with the remembrance of Sita.

Now Ram asked Sugreeva, the reason of his residence in the forest. He told all what had happened with him. He further said that due to fear of Bali my elder brother, I am residing here on the hills. When Ram heard the tragic story of his friend Sugreeva he became very angry. He promised Sugreeva to kill Bali in a single stroke of their arrow. No one in this world could save Bali now. Saying this, Ram told some virtues of a real friend. The real friend is that who sets aside all their great pains of his friends. The real friend should help to escape their friends from bad deeds and should show a good way. At the time of misfortunes the friend should help his friend by all means according to their capacity. If he is sweet speaking and his nature is back biting, it will be good to forget such type of friends. Because they may prove more dangerous like snake, it would be better to leave him. Thus Sri Ram said to Sugreeva that well friend, don't mind for anything. I will try my best to help you. Sugreeva told Sri Ram about the bravery of Bali. But Ram asked him not to be worry for this. And with a little effort Sri Ram killed Bali, when he was fighting with Sugreeva. At the time of death Bali asked Sri Ram that you are almighty God. If you have carnated yourself for the protection of Dharam and to destroy the evil doors from the earth then why you have killed me like a hunter.

धर्म हेतु अवतरेउ गोसाईं।

मारेहु मोहि व्याधि की नाईं॥
Dharma hetu avaterau gosai
Marehu mohi vyadhi ki nayi.

What is the reason of this? You are the father of the whole universe. You are the creator of the world. I am your enemy and Sugreeva is lovable for you. This is not justice. Please tell me my mistake. Ram replied, Listen Bali! if a person looks with bad sense towards the wife of his son, to the wife of his younger brother or to their sister, he is worth killing, because they are equal to daughter. Bali requested Ram that at the time of death I am seeing my Lord. So now I should not die as a sinner. Hearing his tender tone, Ram touched his head from his hands and said, do you want to live more in this world? Bali replied, this is my good luck that you, the God himself is present before me on the time of departure from this world I only beg to get your devotion in every life. At last Bali called his son Angad and gave his hand in the hands of Sri Ram. In this way Bali left this world forever.

Sri Ram sent Bali to his home, the heaven. And when Tara his wife came to know about the death of her husband, she became very sad. When Raghunath saw her in grief, he preached her about Maya and Brahm. He told that this mortal body is made of five things. They are earth, water, fire, sky and wind. This body is perishable but the soul is always immortal. According to Bhagwat Gita:

नैनं छिन्दन्ति शस्त्राणि, नैनं दहति पावकः।
न चैनं क्लेदयन्त्यायो, न शोषयति मारूतः॥

Nainan chindathi shastrani, nainam dehati pavakah.
Na chainam kledayntyayo, na shoshyati marutah.

In this way Tara got enlightenment and she touched the feet of Lord Sri Ram. She asked for devotion only. Then Sri Ram asked Sugreeva to do all his formal duties of his dead brother. He did all according to the custom and tradition of the family. Ram sent Laxman to make Sugreeva the king. He did the same. Sugreeva become the king and Angad became the prince. When Sugreeva asked Ram to reside in the palace, Sri Ram told him that I will not enter in any village or house, till fourteen years. So we will stay on Pravarsan hills.

The gods knew this fact that our Lord Sri Ram would come and reside here for some time, so in advance they had arranged all the necessary things on the hills. The natural beauty was spreading every where. Different types of flowers were filled in the hills and forest. Several fruits were ready for the service of their Lord Sri Ram. There was beauty everywhere. Gradually, the rainy season came. The thundering and lightening of the clouds were very attractive. Ram says to Laxman that the clouds are thundering in the sky and I am feeling fear in the absence of my beloved wife Sita.

दामिनि दमकि रही घन माहि, खल की प्रीति यथा चिर नाहीं।
बरसहिं जलदि भूमि नियराये, यथा नवहिं बुध विद्या पाये॥

Damini damaki rahi ghan mahi, khal ki priti yatha chir nahin.
Barasahin jaladi bhumi niyaraye, yatha navahin budh vidya paye.

Some how the rainy season passed and winter season came. The sky became clear. There were no clouds in the sky. The season became pleasant.

Now Sri Ram thought to move ahead for searching out Sita. With the help of Sugreeva, Hanuman, Angad and Jamwant, they thought out a plan. In the guidance of all these commanders, a huge army was prepared for movement. Sugreeva told them all that if they will come back without searching out Sita, I shall kill you all. So you have to search out Sita anyhow and from anywhere. Thus, they all went in the south direction bowing their heads in the feet of Sri Ram. In the last, when hanuman bowed his head in the feet of Sri Ram, he touched his head, gave his ring and asked him to console Sita. Hanuman thanked his fate and went pleasantly. They were wandering on the hills, in forests, and caves to search out Sita. Whenever, they met the demons in the way, they killed them in a single stroke. Once they entered in a dense forest and forgot the way. In the meantime they felt thirsty. It seemed that they all will die of over pouring thirst. Hanuman climbed on a hill to look for water. He saw a cave where birds and animals were entering and coming out. Hanuman came down from the hill and took everyone to that cave. They all drank water and quenched their thirst.

Now they began to think that how they can search out Sita. All were hopeless. Angad, jamwant, Hanuman and the other commanders were discussing about the way to find out Sita. From the hills Sampati the vulture king heard their voice and came out. He was of a heavy body, all the commanders with the soldiers were afraid to see him. He said, I have been hungry from a long time and God has given me enough food. At a time when Angad talked about the good deeds of the vulture Jatayu, Sampati asked them to tell more about him. They told Sampati that Jatayu had already dedicated himself in the service of Lord Sri Ram. He was luckyone and went to heaven. When Sampati came to know about the death, of his younger brother Jatayu, he became very sad. Though Sampati was unable to move from one place to another because his feathers were burnt with the excessive heat of the sun, yet he asked them to take him to the sea shore, so that he may pay his formal duties for his dead younger brother. They took him to the sea shore on his request. He paid his formal duties by giving water form the sea to console his soul. Then he told them the whole history what had happened with him. He said that when we, the two brothers, were so young, strong and healthy. We flew up to the sun. We went high and high in the sky near the sun. When the heat of the sun became unbearable, my younger brother Jatayu came back to the earth. But due to pride of my power to fly, I did not came back. I flew ahead high and high in the sky. And the result was clear. All of a sudden my feathers began to burn with the excessive heat of the sun. It is said, the excess of everything is bad. So, I found the result of my pride. It was a natural punishment. When my feathers were burnt in the sky, being helpless I fell down on the ground with a cry. There was a Rishi named Chandrama. When he saw me in such a miserable condition, he felt pity on me. He served and cured me. He preached me some religious happenings. He told me that one should not be proud of his big body, because it is but certain that this body which is young today, on getting time it will grow old. And the day will come, when we have to leave the body. So, there is no question to be proud of it. This body is not permanent. Only soul is permanent and immortal. One should never proud of it. Thus, by the preachings of Rishi chandrama, my proudness turned into devotion.

At that time, the Rishi foretold me that in Tretayug the God Himself will carnate in the form of a man. The demon being Ravan will kidnap his wife. And in search of his wife, he will send the ambassadors. You have to show them Sita from your place and your feathers will grow again undoubtedly. Sampati said, that the words of the Rishi Chandrama were going to be true today. You all the ambassadors of Sri Ram met me and now I am very thankful to all of you. I feel that by the mercy of God Sri Ram, you will get success in your aim. You will get to know about Sita.

He said, there is a country name Lanka at the hill of Trikoot. It is an Island. This country is surrounded by the oceans from all sides. There resides the demon king Ravan fearlessly. Now Sita is sitting in Ashok Vatika in Lanka. She is in a thinking Mood. Actually she looks very sad. I am seeing her but you cannot see her because my eye sight is so strong than you.

मैं देख हूँ तुम नाहीं, गीघही दृष्टि अपार।
बूढ भयउं न त करतेउं, कछुक सहाय तुम्हार॥

Main dekh hun tum nahin, ghigahi drishti apar.
Boodh bhayaun na ta karateun, kachuka sahay tumhar.

I was in favour to help you, but I am grown old. So, how can I help You? Sampati told him the way to go to lanka. He said, the person will cross the seven seas, only he may do something for Ram. Please see me. It is the mercy of Lord Sri Ram that had made me like this. Now I am so healthy due to the God's grace. If a sinner remembers his name, he may go across the Bhawasagar. And you people are the devotees of Sri Ram. You please do not loose heart. Do your duty as you could. Saying this the vulture king went away. They all were wondered to see this.

Every one said, I can cross the sea, but it is hard to return back from there safely. The Jamwant said that now I have become so old. There is no power in my body. Jamwant said, when God tied Bali and made their body high upto the sky I took two rounds of Him. Angad said, I may cross the sea, but returning may be difficult for me. Then jamwant reminded Hanuman of his inherent power. He told Hanuman that you were the centre of wisdom, knowledge and science. You have the extraordinary power like wind.

पवन तनय बल पवन समाना।
का चुप साधि रहेउ बलवाना॥

Pawan tanay bal pawan samana.
Ka chup sadhi raheu balwana.

Then why have you become silent? There is no work in the world which you can not do. You are only born to do work of Lord Sri Ram. Hearing these words of Jamwant, Hanuman made his physical feature so huge like a mountain. His body became so heavy. He roared like the lion. He said now I can go across the ocean in a playing mood. Hanuman asked to Jamwant to tell him the proper way and to give him the best suggestion. He said now I can bring here the whole Lanka. I can kill the demon king Ravan with all of his army. He said that a handful of the demons have no courage to face me. Jamwant suggested Hanuman to go Lanka to see if Sita is there or not. If it is so, please come back with the information of Sita. Further Sri Ram himself will do according to their programme.

Sri Ram will bring Sita after killing the whole demon generation. And the Rishies and Munies will sing song in their devotion throughout the whole universe. Thus, Goswami Tulsidas says that the person who says and understands the themes of his devotion, he begets the Moksha, the Param pad. His name is greater than of himself.

Goswami Tulsidas measures the distinction between the power of Sri Ram and the power of their name on the balance of reasoning rod. At last he comes to the conclusion that, his name is hundred times more powerful than he himself. Goswamiji further says that even Sri Ram himself cannot describe the dignity of their power.

कहँ लगि करउं मै नाम बडाई।
राम न सकहिं नाम गुण गाई॥
राम एक तापस तिय तारी।
नाम कोटि खल कुमति सुधारी॥
नाम लेत भव सिन्धु सुखाहीं।
करहुँ विचार सुजन मन माही॥
राम राम कहि जे जमुहाहीं।
ते कोटिक अध पुंज नसाहीं॥

Kahn lagi karaun mein naam badai,
Ram na sakahin naam gun gayi.
Ram ek tapas tiya tari,
Naam koti khal kumati sudhari.
Naam leth bhav sindhu sukhahin,
Karahu vichar sujan man mahi.
Ram Ram kahi je jamuhahin,
Te kotik adh punj nasahi.

Vibhishan in The Feet Of Sri Ram

O God! hearing your name and fame I have surrendered in your feet. I have come for shelter to you. Please be kind and let me serve in your feet.

श्रवन सुयस सुनि आयउं, प्रभु भंजन भव भीर।
त्राहि त्राहि आरत हरन, सरन सुखद रघुवीर॥

Shrawan sujas suni ayaun,
Prabhu bhanjan bhwa bheer.
Trahi Trahi arat haran,
Saran sukhad Raghubir.

Chapter 5
SUNDER KAND

In this Kand Goswami Tulsidas first of all worships Lord Sri Ram who is the creator and father of the world, and who purifies our mind from many evils. After that he prays to Hanumanji who is the centre of all virtues and who is the most lovable devotee of Lord Sri Ram.

Hearing the worlds of Jamwant, Sri Hanumanji became very pleased. He told everyone of his company that they have to wait for him until he does not return from Lanka taking the welfare of Sitaji. Saying this he hurriedly climbed up a hill. He remembered Sri Raghubir and jumped and crossed the ocean. In the mid of the ocean, Mountain Mainak raised from the water level and asked Hanuman to take a little rest. But Hanuman said that without doing the pious work of Sri Ram, how I can take rest.

'राम काज कीन्हे बिना, मोहि कहाँ विश्राम'
Ram kaj kinhe bina, mohi kahan vishram.

When gods saw Hanuman going across the sea, they tried to know the capability of Hanumanji. They sent Sursa to test Hanuman. On the way to Lanka, she came before Hanuman. She opened her mouth like a cave. Hanumanji became double than her. When she opened her mouth for about hundred miles, now Hanumanji came in a very short from and entered in her mouth. When he came out from her mouth, Sursa blessed Hanumanji. She said, you will succeed in your aim without any hesitation. No one can dare to check your way.

राम काज सब करिहुं, तुम्ह बल बुद्धि निधान।
आसिष देह गई सो, हरषि चलेउ हनुमान॥
Ram kaj sab karihun, tumh bal buddhi nidhan
Aasish deh gayi so, harashi chaleu Hanuman.

Now he marched ahead towards his aim. It was the set up of Ravan that by airways also, no one could cross the sea. For this, he had deputed a demon like Radar in the ocean to watch up the airways. In this way, when Hanuman was crossing the sea, it captured the reflection of Hanuman in the sea water and thus, he was unable to fly ahead. Hanumanji knew the reason of this and he killed the demon of water and reached on the ground of Lanka. There he saw the natural beauty of the hills and forest. Different types of animals and birds were chattering in the forests. Hanuman climbed up a hill, from where he saw the construction of Lanka. He saw that it was made like a special type of fort surrounded by sea from all sides. He also saw that many soldiers of heavy body were guarding Lanka on the main spots. When he saw a large number of guards on their duty, he thought within himself that he should take very short form of his body to enter in the city of Ravan.

Hanuman made the form of a mosquito. Remembering Lord Sri Ram, he entered into Lanka. A lady demon named Lankini, at once, saw Hanuman and stood in his way, because she was the most intelligent guard of Ravan. She challenged Hanuman that no one could escape from her eyes. At this Hanuman beat her by his hand on her jawa. He gave her a blow. Blood began to flow from her mouth. Now she thought that the last time of demon generation has come. She prayed Hanuman and asked him to go to Lanka to do his duty remembering Lord Sri ram. Here, Goswami Tulsidas says that the poison becomes nectar, the enemy behaves like a friend, the ocean may come in the feet of the cow, the fire may become cold, the mountain can become little like a grain of sand. The above thing may be possible only when Sri Ram will see any one wit merciful eyes. His mercy can make impossible things possible. It depends on us that how much mercy we may get from him.

Now Hanuman made his smallest feature of a mosquito again and entered in Lanka. He touched every spot but could not find Sita. Thus, separate from all, he saw a house which was out of residence. The house was decorated with Ramayan. There was a small plant of Tulsi at the gate, which was indication that the house was of a devotee not of the cruel demon. Thus, seeing the house of a devotee in Lanka Hanuman became very pleased. He began to think within himself that Lanka is the country of demons, how a gentle man came here. In the meantime, Vibhishan woke up and started saying Ram! Ram!

लंका निसिचर निकर निकसा, इहां कहां सज्जन कर वासा।
मनमहं तरक करन कपि लागा, तेहि समय विभिषन तागा॥

राम राम तेहि सुमिरन कीन्हा, हृदय हरषि कपि सज्जन चीन्हा।
एहिं सन हठ करिहउं पहिचानी, साधु ते होइ न कारज हानी॥

Lanka nishchir nikar nikasa, ihan kahan sajjan kar vasa.
Manmahn tarak karan kapi laga, tehi samay Vibhishan taga.
Ram Ram tehi sumiran kinha, hriday harashi kapi sajjan chinha.
Aehin san hath karihun pahichani, sadhu te hoyi na karaj hani.

Hanuman thought that I should contact this fellow and it will be favourable for me. He called Vibhishan in the form of a Brahman. When he heard some one calling at the door Vibhishan came out and asked his welfare after salution. Now Vibhishan wanted to know his address. Then Hanuman told him all about Sri Ram and his name. Hearing this felt inner pleasure. Vibhishan told Hanuman that he was living in Lanka like the tongue lives in between teeth.

सुनहुं पवनसुत रहनि हमारी, जिमि दसनन्ह महं जीभि विचारी।
तात कबहुँ मोहि जानि अनाथा, करिहहिं कृपा भानुकुल नाथा।
अब मोहि भा भरोस हनुमंता, विनुहरि कृपा मिलइ नहिं संता॥

Sunahun Pawansut rahani hamari, jimi dasannah mahn jhibhi vichari.
Tat kabahun mohi jani anatha, karihahin krupa bhanukul natha.
Ab mohi bha bharos Hanumantha, vinuhari krupa milai nahin santha.

Well Pawansut, thinking of me as a sinner and an orphan, Raghunath will ever shower and pour his mercy on me. It is the grace of Lord Raghubir that you met me. Hanuman replied, I am not born in a high family, I also don't belong to human race, if any one takes my name early in the morning it is a fact that he will not get food on that very day. Though I am a wild creature only Sri Ram has bestowed his mercy on me. Saying this tears appeared in the eyes of Hanuman.

Further Hanuman said that knowing the gentle nature of such a master, if any body forgets him, there is no doubt that he would have to suffer a lot. Thus, describing the gentleness of Sri Ram he got a great pleasure. Then Vibhishan told all about Sita and told him the way to meet her. He again came in the form of a mosquito and went into Ashok Vatika, where Sita was sitting under a Ashok tree. Seeing the miserable condition of Sita, he became very sad.

कृष्ण तन सीस जटा इक बेनी, जपत हृदय रघुपति गुन श्रेनी।
Krish tan sees jata ika beni, japat hriday raghupati gun shreni.

He hid himself in between the leaves and branches, and began to think about his programme, what to do and what not to do. This question was striking the mind of Hanuman again and again. In the meantime, Ravan came there with a great pomp and show. That duffer fellow tried his best to pacify Sita by all means and said, if you agree with me all the queens of Lanka with Mandodri will accept your service. So please look at me only once. Sita called him names and said angrily, you shameless fellow, you have stolen me, when I was all alone there in the ashram. You need not worry. Sri Ram will take your care very soon by his arrow. At this Ravan became very angry. He asked some women demons to torture Sita. Saying this he went to his residence. The leader of those women was Trijata. She was the devotee of Sri Ram. She forbade her companions not to do so. And told them about her dream which she had seen last night. She told them that in the dream I have seen that a monkey has burnt the whole Lanka and had killed a lot of army of the demons. Sri Ram has won the battle and he had called on Sita with love. She further told that I am firm about my dream that it will become true within few days. Hearing this statement of Trijata, everyone of them shivered with fear and they all began to touch the feet of Sita.

त्रिजटा नाम राक्षसी एका, राम चरन रति निपुन विवेका।
सबलौ बोलि सुनायसि सपना, सीतहिं सेइ करहुँ हित अपना॥
Trijata naam rakshasi Eka, Ram charan rati vipun Viveka.
Sablau boli sunayasi sapna, sitahin seyi karahun hit apna.

When they all went away, Sita began to think within herself that Ravan will kill me after one month and she became very sad. Hanuman dropped the ring from the tree before Sita. Sita was astonished to see the ring of Sri Ram. She thought that no one in the world can dare to win Lord Ram then how and from where this ring has come here. Such type of ring can not be Maya (illusion). Now Hanuman came down from the tree went to Sita and touched her feet. Telling his address he told that I have come from Ram. Touching the feet of Sri Ram I say that I have brought this ring to you given by Sri Ram. He told all about the friendship of Sugreeva with Sri Ram. When she finally knew that the fellow is a devotee of Sri Ram by body, mind and soul then tears appeared in her eyes. She said to Hanuman that you have become a ship in the ocean for me. Seeing her sadness, Hanuman spoke in a sweet tone that, our Lord Sri Ram is completely well with his younger brother Laxman. He is sad only for you. You please never think otherwise. There is a greater place for you in the heart of Sri Ram. Now please listen to the message of Sri Ram.

Sri Ram has said that in your absence, in your separation, all the things of pleasure have become troublesome. Only my heart knows the secret of love between I and you. And that very heart always lives with you. Hearing the message of Sri Ram the heart of Sita filled with gratitude towards Hanuman said, well mother! You need not worry. You please remember Sri Ram by heart. You just imagine that the demons are about to die. They have invited their death.

I can take you with me just now, but Sri Ram has not ordered me to do so. Well mother! You please wait for some time, Sri Ram will come here with a huge army. He will kill the demons and take you with him. Sita asked Hanuman that tell me about the army of Sri Ram because the demons appear so brave, I feel suspense within myself. To clear the suspense of Sita, Hanuman became titan. He stood before her like a rock. His physical features was like a scort. When she saw the huge body of Hanuman, she was satisfied. Then he came in his original form. Thinking of him as the devotee of Sri Ram she blessed him to become immortal. Hanuman bowed his head again in her feet and said my mother now I am fully satisfied by your blessing. He requested to mother Sita that I am very hungry. Let me eat these lovely fruits. She said, dear son, this garden is being guarded by brave demons. How would you succeed in eating this fruits? He said if you permit me mother to go there, I do not fear these demons. She saw him wise and powerful so she allowed him to eat the fruits remembering the feet of Sri Ram. He touched her feet and entered into the garden. He ate fruits and began to break the plants and trees. When the guards opposed him, he killed them. Some of them escaped themselves and went to the court of demon king Ravan. They told Ravan all about the bravery of the monkey. They said that a fearful monkey has come in the garden. He has eaten all the fruits and had broken many plants. They further said that when we opposed him, he killed many of us.

Ravan send his son Akshay Kumar to face the monkey. Hanuman broke a heavy tree and threw it on him. Akshay Kumar was crushed and died under the tree. The monkey crushed many of those demons by his legs and hands. Some of them again went to Ravan and told him about the death of his son, he got very angry. He sent Meghnad his elder son to tie and bring the monkey alive. He asked him not to kill the monkey. Ravan had a great faith on the bravery of Meghnad because he had defeated even Indra, the king of gods, in the battlefield. So he was called Indrajeet. Indrajeet went there angrily, because he was very sad on the death of his younger brother. When the monkey saw that some heavy demon is coming towards him. He challenged him with a loud laughter. The monkey took a heavy tree and threw it on the chariot of Indrajeet. Thus, his chariot was ruined his horses died. Now they began to fight each other like an elephant. Indrajeet tried his best but could not win Anjani Kumar, because he was beyond his reach. Thus, at last he used his Brahamastra.

ब्रम्ह अस्त्र तेहि साध कपिमन कीन्ह विचार।
जौ न ब्रह्म सर मानउँ महिमा मिटै अपारा॥

Brahma astra tehi sadha kapiman kinha vichar.
Jo na Brahma sar mahaun mahima mitai apar.

Now the (Hanuman) thought within himself that if I will not honour to this very Brahamastra then its grace will decrease. So in honour of Brahamastra, he became senseless. Thus, Indrajeet tied him in Nagpash and presented him before his father. When the demons came to know about the monkey, they reached the court to see him. Hanuman saw the grand court of Ravan, which was praiseworthy. There all the gods were standing in order to follow the command of Ravan. But the monkey was so fearless in between the demons like the Garud bird sits fearlessly between the snakes.

देखि प्रताप न कपि मन संका।
जिमि अहिगन मँह गरूड असंका॥

Dekhi pratap na kapi man sanka.
Jimi ahigan mhan Garud asanka.

When Ravan saw the monkey in such a fearless mood, he called his name and laughed. And thinking about the death of his son he became sad.

Ravan the demon king enquired, well monkey, who are you? How have you come here? You have not heard about me. You seem very fearless. Why have you killed the demons? What was their fault? You could not mind for your life. The monkey replied gently. He said, well Ravan listen, I am the ambassador of that person who has made this whole universe, who carnates himself to kill the evil doors like you and to console the ailing humanity, who had broken the bow of Lord Shiva in the Swayambar of Sita at Janakpur, who had killed the bravest demons like Khar, Dooshan, Trishra and Bali with a little effort. He further told that I am the ambassador of that person whose wife you have stolen. Well Ravan I know well about your bravery. There is nothing to say for you.

I was so hungry. I ate some fruits in your garden. The guards beat me so I killed them. Everyone try to save himself so there is nothing like fault by my side. Yes, your son has tied me in vein. But I am not ashamed that your son has tied me, because I wish to do the work of my Lord. He requested Ravan to follow the preaching by setting his proud aside. He told that you belong to a high Brahman family. Which is respected by the whole world so leave the delusion and go to the feet of Lord Sri Ram who is the protector of his devotees. Actually he is that supreme power, to whom the death himself feels fear, who eats all the worldly creatures. So never make enemity of him. You please mind for my request and give back Janki to him. He further said that Sri Ram is very kind by nature. And if you will surrender yourself towards him, he will excuse you for your faults. Hanuman suggested him to go in the feet of Sri Ram and to lead a very prosperous and long life. He requested him not to become a blot on the fair name of Rishi Pulasti. He requested him to think twice that the tongue is worthless if it does not say Ram! Ram! He challenged that even Lord Shiva, Lord Vishnu and Bramha also cannot protect the opponent of Lord Sri Ram. So please mind for my request, the love, the illusion is very troublesome. Thus, leave the proud and go in to the feet of Sri Ram because he is the ocean of mercy.

Though the monkey had advised him for his welfare but he did not like it because of his pride. So he laughed and said, I have gotten a very good monkey as a teacher. You are about to die so you have started preaching me. Hanuman replied, it will go its opposite. Your mind is disturbed. You are unable to think of your good. He felt ashamed at this and ordered his soldiers to kill the monkey immediately. The demons rushed at him but in the meantime his younger brother Vibhishan came there. He bowed low and requested him not to kill the ambassador, because it is against the general rule. He suggested them to punish the monkey in any other way. Everybody agreed at this suggestion. They came to the conclusion to role some clothes on the tail of the monkey and to dip it with oil and burn it. When the Hanuman heard all these, he thought that mother Saraswati is favourable for me now.

The demons arranged a lot of clothes from the whole country, because the monkey had raised his tail so long. There was a great gathering to see this all. People were beating drums and clapping cheers. They made a procession and then burnt the tail, he jumped and ran his burning tail, on the roofs of the palace. The wives of the demons were frightened to see such a scene. By the mercy of God forty-nine type of winds began to blow. Hanuman roared and raised his body high to the sky. He jumped from one building to another. In this way the golden Lanka began to burn. The flames of fire were touching the sky. He burnt the whole country in a short time. Only the house of Vibhishan was saved, because he was the devotee of Sri Ram.

जारा नगर निमिष एक माहीं एक विभीषन कर गृह नाहीं।
ताकर दूत अनल जेहि सिरिजा, जरान सो तेहि कारन गिरिजा॥
Jara nagar nimish ek mahin, ek Vibhiskan kar grih nahin.
Takar doot anal hehi sirija, jaran so tehi karan girija.

He burnt Lanka from every corner and then he jumped into the sea. Now he stood before Sitaji and bowed his head in her feet.

पूँछि बुझाइ खोह श्रम धरि लघु रूप बहोरि।
जनक सुता के आगे, ठाढ़ भयउ कर जोरि॥
Punchi bhujai khoh shram dhari laghu roop bahori,
Janak suta ke aage, tadh bhayau kar jori.

Hanuman requested Sitaji to give some presentation from her side to Sri Ram as he had given you his ring. Sita gave her Churamani to present to Sri Ram in exchange. Hanuman took it pleasantly. Now she said him to convey her salutation in the feet of Sri Ram. Sita told that if Sri Ram will not come to take her from here within the month, he will not see her alive. Well Hanuman! You were the only base for me here and now you are also ready to go leaving me alone in Lanka. How I can be alive here. When I saw you, I was much satisfied, but now the day and night, pleasure and pain both will be same for me. Hanuman tried his best to pacify Sita and went to Sri Ram after touching the feet of Mother Sita.

When he left Lanka, he roared in such a way, by which the pregnant woman of the demons community became abortioned. He came back across the sea and laughed loudly in his manner.

When his companions, heard the voice of Hanuman they thought that our Hanuman has come back. They met each other, they felt pleasure in the same way as the fish feels pleasure on getting water, being out of water for a long time. They went to Sri Ram asking and telling about what had happened. When Sri Ram saw that all the monkeys are coming towards him happily with their king Sugreeva. He thought that the work has been done. Now they sat on a smooth and white stone. All the monkeys came there and touched the feet of Sri Ram one by one. Sri Ram met them with great affection and asked their welfare. Jamwant said to Ragunathji that the person on whom you are merciful, he will be always good and he will get victory in every walk of life. Jamwant further said that our work has been done by your mercy and our life has become thankful. Jamwant told Sri Ram about the good deeds of Hanuman, what he had done. Sri Ram became very glad and then he embraced Hanumanji. Sri Ram asked Hanuman that how Sita lives and protect there herself.

Hanuman told Sri Ram that she has the only base of your name. She remembers Ram! Ram! day and night. On my departure she has given me her Churamani and he presented it before him. Raghupati took it and touched it from his heart. And he asked the welfare of Sita again and again. Hanuman told that even a single moment for her is passing like thousands of years. So now we should go there to take her without any delay. Hearing about the miserable condition of Sita, tears appeared in the eyes of Sri Ram. It is the matter of wonder that the God himself is feeling sad while he is beyond pleasure and pain. His heart was filled with gratitude towards the deeds of Hanuman. He said to Hanuman that there is nothing with me to reply you or to give you in response. Now Hanuman bowed low in the feet of Sri Ram. He took Hanuman in his arms and beseated him by his side and asked him that the fort of the Lanka is invulnerable then how have you crossed it? And how you have burnt the whole Lanka? When Hanuman saw that his Lord is pleased on him, he told all what had happened in Lanka. But he said that this is all due to your grace. I had no power to do anything. Hanuman said that nothing is impossible in this world for that person, on whom you are merciful. Because by your grace a single flame of fire can burn the whole ocean within no time.

Now Hanuman asked Sri Ram to give him his Upnayani devotion in response. Parvatiji says to Shiva that the person who knew the polite nature of Lord Ram, he will never ask for anything inspite of devotion. Only that person can get devotion of

Sri Ram who thinks and sings this conversation. Thus, Sri Ram called Sugreeva to prepare the whole army. Now a huge army was prepared to march towards Lanka. Every soldier touched the feet of Sri Ram and he blessed them all. By getting the mercy of Sri Ram they got extraordinary power.

राम कृपा बल पाइ कपिन्दा, भये पच्छ युत मनहुँ गिरिन्दा।
राम कृपा अतुलित बल तिनही, तृन समान त्रैलोकहिं गनहीं॥

Ram kripa bal payi kapinda, bhaye pachchh yut manahu girinda.
Ram kripa atulit bal tinhi, trin saman triyilokahin ganahi.

Ram started towards Lanka pleasantly. It seemed that all the stars were favourable for him. When Janki came to know about the movement of Sri Ram Prabhu, her left hand began to vibrate. The huge army of vanars and bears marched ahead. The soldiers were roaring like the lion. The army was so huge that on its movement the earth began to move. After some time the army reached on the shore of ocean. The brave soldiers began to eat fruits here and there.

There in Lanka, the demons were frightened by the doings of Hanuman, when he had burnt Lanka. Everybody in Lanka was thinking that now our good days have gone. If their ambassador was so strong and brave then what is to say about the bravery of Sri Ram. Mandodari herself was in grief, Mandodari was a goddess. She requested her husband to give up Sita, if he wants the welfare of the family. She said that if you would not give back Sita then even Shankar Bhagwan and Brahma also can not protect you. So let us lead a happy live. And you please give back Sita to Sri Ram with honour and respect. Due to proudness Ravan did not heed the request of his queen Mandodari. He laughed loudly and said, if the monkeys will come across the sea, our poor and hungry demons will eat them up. You know well that the whole world is shivering by my name, and being my queen you are feeling fear like an ordinary woman. It is not good for you. Mandodary thought within herself that nature has become unkind on my husband and due to this he is talking like this. On the other day, when he sat in his court a messenger told him that the army of Sri Ram has come across the sea. Ravan asked his courtiers and discussed on the present situation. He asked them what to do and what not to do. They laughed and said, you need not worry please. You have won Indra with a little effort and these men, monkeys and bears have no values at all. All these are our food.

It is said that if these three personalities like minister, doctor and Guru speaks sweet due to fear, it is sure that the king's three things - kingdom, religion, and body will go ruin.

सचिव वैद्य गुरू तीनि जौं, प्रिय बोलहिं भय आस।
राज, धर्म, तन तीनि कर, होहिं वेगिही नास।
सोइ रावण कहुँ बनी सहाई, अस्तुति करहि सुनाई सुनाई॥

Sachiv vaidya guru teeni jaun, priya bolahin bhaya aas.
Raj, dhram, tan teeni kar, hohin vehgihi naas.
Soi Ravan kahun bani sahai, astuti karahi sunai sunai.

And it was the same situation for Ravan. On getting good time his younger brother Vibhishan came there in his court. He bowed his head and requested his brother to leave other's wife because such type of deeds will be a blot on our family. He told Ravan about Sri Ram and Laxman that they are not ordinary men. He is the Lord of the world and universe. He is Brahma the God. He is present in every particle of the world. He is endless. He is invincible. He never takes birth and never die He is omnipresent. He has carnated himself in the form of man, for the welfare of cows, Brahman, earth and gods.

He is born for the protection of vedas and Dharma. Whose name is sufficient to ruin three types of troubles they are physical, natural and worldly, that God has taken birth. So, I am touching your feet again and again and I request you to leave your proudness and go in the feet of Sri Ram. Rishi Pulasti our grandfather has also send this message which I have requested. Malyawant an old and wise minister of his court also agreed with Vibhishan. Ravan became angry on both of them and kicked them from the court. He did not mind for their request. He angrily asked Vibhishan to go to Ram whom he was praising and praising. Ravan kicked Vibhishan and asked him to get out from the palace.

Now Vibhishan went in the feet of Sri Ram. On the way he was thinking and willing to see his own Lord Sri Ram. Thinking like this he came across the sea. When the monkeys saw an stranger coming towards their camp they thought him to be their enemy. So they took him to Sugreeva. Sugreeva informed Sri Ram about the reaching of Vibhishan the brother of Ravan in their camp. Sri Ram ordered Sugreeva to present Vibhishan before him. Vibhishan was presented before Sri Ram. When he saw the charming face of the Lord from a distance he was wonder-struck. Vibhishan gave their address to Sri Ram that, Sir I am the brother of Dashanan the demon king of Lanka. I have born in a cruel demon family. By nature I am a sinner. As an owl always likes darkness in the same way sin is my birth right. I have heard enough about your kind nature, so now my whole life is in your feet.

श्रवन सुयस सुनि आयउँ, प्रभु भंजन भव भीर।
त्राहि त्राहि आरत हरन, सरन सुखद रघुवीर॥
अस कहि करत दण्डवत देखा, तुरत उठे प्रभु हरष विसेखा॥

Shravan suyas suni aayaun, Prabhu bhanjan bhav bheer.
Trahi trahi aarat haran, saran sukhad Raghuvir.
Asa kahi karat dandavat dekha, turat uthe Prabhu harash visekha.

Sri Ram saw that Vibhishan has surrendered himself in my feet, so he welcomed him warmly. He asked his welfare. He told, my Lord, I am residing in a wrong atmosphere. My surrounding is filled with wrong and notorious people, so how I can follow the principles of religion. Vibhishan said, it is good to live in the hell, but to live in the company of wrong and notorious people is not good.

बरू भल बास नरक कर ताता।
दुष्ट संग जानि देह विधता॥

Baru bhal bas narak kar tatha.
Dushta sang jaani deh vidhata.

He said all type of evils reside in the heart of people until they do not remember Raghunath. Now seeing your feet, all type of evil thoughts have gone away. It is my good luck and it is your grace that I saw your feet, which is beyond the reach of great saints and sages.

Sri Ram made him his friend and said, only Kag Bhushandi knew this secret of my nature. Listen my friend the person who had done enemity from the whole world and from every creature if he comes to me without any pride, I shall accept him as my devotee. Such type of people are lovable for me in the same way as the miser loves his money. And you are like a saint, your behaviour is like a saint so you have become part and partial to me. When the monkeys heard such sweet words of Sri Ram they began to say Jai Sri Ram. And when Vibhishan heard these polite words of Sri Ram his heart filled with gratitude. He requested him to give his pious devotion which they have given to Lord Shiva. Sri Ram, at once, understood the sense of their devotee. He said, as you like, you will get and asked for sea water. Sri Ram said, though you are not willing for this, but yet I am making you the king of Lanka. Saying this he made a pious red mark on his forehead. The gods showered flowers from the sky.

Though Sri Ram is almighty yet he asked ocean to give the way. He went to the ocean and bowed their head towards him. He prayed the ocean.

When Vibhishan came to Sri Ram, Ravan sent two ambassadors named Suk and Sarang to spy on him. When Suk and Sarang saw the kind behaviour of Sri Ram in disguise they forgot everything and came in their original form. They began to praise the gentle nature of Lord Sri Ram. When the monkeys saw the ambassadors of the enemy, they took him to Sugreeva. The monkeys began to beat him, some by kegs and some by hands. They cried for the help of Sri Ram, Laxman forbade them not to do so. Laxman wrote a letter to give it to Ravan. Suk and Sarang returned to Lanka.

The ambassador came to Ravan and saluted him. Seeing them Ravan laughed and asked their welfare. Suk and Sarang told him that your younger brother Vibhishan met Sri Ram. They have made him the king of Lanka by putting a pious red mark on his forehead. As far as the question of the strength of his army is concerned I have heard that there are eighteen Padum chief commanders in that army. They reported that:

अस मै श्रवन सुना दसंकघर, पदुम अठारह जूथप बन्दर।
नाथ कटक मँह कोउ अस नाहीं, जो तुमहि जीतहि रन माहीं॥
परम क्रोध मीजहिं सब हाथा, आयसु पै न देहिं रघुनाथा।
गर्जहिं तर्जहिं सहज असंका, मानहुं ग्रसन चहत हैं लंका॥

Asa mein shravan suna dasankghar, padum atharah joothap bandar.
Nath katak mah kou asa nahi, jo tumahi jitahi run mahin.
Param krodh mijahin sab hatha, aayasu pey na dehi Rahunatha.
Garjahin tarjahin sahaj asanka, manahun grasan chahat hein Lanka.

The monkey who had burnt your Lanka was a simple runner of Sugreeva. As I have seen, their soldiers are so strong that even you cannot win with him in the struggle. They are completely ready to attack on Lanka, but Sri Ram is not giving him permission to do so. They are roaring and willing to eat up Lanka. Among them, Sri Ram is so powerful that even thousands of Shesh Nag can no describe his bravery. His younger brother Laxman had given a letter to you. They presented the letter given by Laxman. He read the letter and laughed loudly about the matter of the letter but was entirely frightened.

Ram prayed the ocean for three days but he did not heed for

their request. Goswami Tulsidas says:

विनय न मानत जलदि जड़, गये तीन दिन बीती।
बोले राम सकोपि तब, भय बिनु होइ न प्रीति॥

Vinay na manat jaladi jadh, gaye teen din beeti.
Bole Ram sakopi tab, bhay binu hoyi na priti.

Sri Ram looked towards Laxman and said:

लाछिमन वान सरासन आनू, सोषौ वारिधि विसिषि कृषानँ।
सठ सन विनय कुटिलसन प्रीति, सहज कृपनसन सुन्दर नीति॥

Laxman vaan sarasan aanu, soshou varidhi visishi krishan.
Sath san vinay kutilasan priti, sahaj kripnasan sunder niti.

Then Sri Ram said angrily, that nobody loves anyone without fear. He asked Laxman to bring his bow and arrow to suck the ocean. Saying this, as Sri Ram took his bow in his hands, the water of the ocean began to boil and the creatures of the ocean began die of its heat. Now the ocean came before Sri Ram in the form of a Brahman with a presentation. Goswami Tulsidasji very remarkably says that the persons who are of a evil nature they do not understand anything by request. They only understand it by punishment and torture. In this way the ocean was frightened and touched the feet of Sri Ram. It begged pardon to Ram and said that sky, wind, fire, water and earth, all these five things are undone. Their activities are undone. These have no feelings and I am among one of your creations. So I should follow you and I shall follow you as you will say. I have to obey you my Lord. The ocean fell down in the feet of Sri Ram.

Sri Ram smiled at the gentle and polite words of the ocean and asked him to arrange such way by which the whole army may go across the sea. The ocean thought a little and made a proposal to Sri Ram. He told that in your army there are two well known engineers. They are Nal and Neel. In their childhood they got blessing by a Rishi that the stone touched by him will swim on the surface of the water. In this way they will throw the stones in the water and I shall also do my best to make a bridge on the ocean. Thus, he told him the method of making a bridge on the surface of the water and pleasantly went away to their home.

In this way the character of Lord Sri Ram is pious and useful for every walk of life for everyone. And the persons who sing and listen to the pious character of Sri Ram they go across the

Bhawasagar without the ship.
Indra's Chariot For Sri Ram

Indra sent a heavenly chariot
on which

Sri Ram rode pleasantly.
Chapter 6
LANKA KAND

On Behalf of the suggestion of the ocean, Sri Ram asked their courtiers to do something to make the bridge over the surface of the water without any delay. Because the whole army has to go across the ocean. Jamwant the experience hand courtier stood and said that Nal and Neel are sufficient as a guide for us. So he called all the bears and monkeys to bring heavy stone from the hills. They did the same. They began to bring the stones and used to give it to Nal and Neel. Nal and Neel began to write the name of Ram on the stones and the monkeys began to throw it in the water. In this way the stones on which Ram word was written they were floating on the surface of the water. Thus, Nal and Neel started the construction of bridge on the water surface of the ocean. Within few days the bridge was prepared. When Sri Ram saw the beautiful construction of the bridge, he laughed with pleasure. He made a proposal to establish the statue of Lord Shiva at this place before departure of the army. Because Lord Shiva is most honourable and respectable for me than anything in the world. Thus, he established the statue of Lord Shiva under the guidance of great saint and sages at Rameshwaram.

मोरे हृदय परम कल्पना।
करिहउँ इहाँ सम्भु थापना॥
Morey hriday param kalpana,
Karihaun Ihan sambhu thapna.

He further said that Lord Shiva and I both are part and parcel to each other. So if anyone loves Lord Shiva and not me and he who loves me and not Lord Shiva, he will have to live in the hell for many lives.

संकर प्रिय मम द्रोही, सिव द्रोही मम दास।
ते नर करहिं कलप भरि, घोर नरक मँह बास॥
Sankar priya mama drohi, Siv drohi mma das.

Te nar karahin kalpa bhari, ghor narak mahn bas.

He told the people that the person who will come to see Lord Shiva at Rameshwaram, he will go to heaven after leaving this body. Everybody was much pleased to hear these words of Lord Sri Ram. Thus, the Rishies and Munies went away to their ashram. Though the bridge was made due to God's grace, due to mercy of Sri Ram, but it is his greatness that he gave name and fame to Nal-Neel and declared that the bridge is built by Nal-Neel.

Now the bridge was completely ready. When Sri Ram saw it, he appreciated its grandness. He ordered the whole army to go across the ocean through the bridge. Thus, Sri ram and Laxman with all of their army came across the sea and made their camps on the shore. Sri Ram ordered them to eat the fruits whatever they get on the trees. The fact is this that all the tress were full of fruits.

When Ravan came to know that, Ram has made the bridge on the surface of the ocean and he has come across the ocean with all of their army, he was entirely frightened. Mandodari also came to know about the reaching of Sri Ram in Lanka. Mandodari tried her best to convince her husband to give back Sita to Sri Ram. She told Ravan that he is not an ordinary man. If he will go before a lion, he will not eat him. Actually he is almighty. He is Kaushalyadheesh Raghuraya. He has come here to shower mercy on you. So please mind For my request and through this your name and fame will remain in this world for a long time . Then Ravan took Mandodari in his arms and said, you need not worry. There is no rival of me in the whole world. All the gods are under my control. So there is no question to get fear with such an ordinary man. His son also tried to forbade him but in vain.

In the evening Ravan sat on the high hills with all of his courtiers to see and hear the musical song and dance. The actresses were dancing and singing there. Though a huge army of the enemy was ready to fight against him but he was totally careless for that. It seemed that he had no fear of all these. On the other hand Sri Ram sat at a smooth stone on a hill with Hanuman, Vibhishan and Laxman also sat there with his bow in his hand to guard his elder brother. When Sri Ram saw in the south direction. He asked Vibhishan that the clouds are thundering and there is flash of lightening in the south. It seems that very soon it may rain cats and dogs. Vibhishan replied to Sri Ram there is neither cloud nor lightening in the sky, but on the hills of Lanka, Ravan is sitting in his company of singers and dancers. The black shed of his throne seems like black clouds. And the ornaments of his queen Mandodari are shining like the lightening in the sky. The sound of the drums appears to be the thunder of the cloud. Then Sri Ram raised his bow and left an arrow which cut the throne, crown and ear ring in a stroke.

छत्र मुकुट तांटक सब, हते एक ही बान।
सबके देखत महि परे, मरमु न काहू जान॥
Chatra mukut tantak sab, hata ek hi baan.
Sabke dekhat mahi pare, marmu na kahu jaan.

Everyone saw that they fell down on the earth but nobody could understand the secret of this. Doing this task the arrow of Sri Ram came back to him. All of the courtiers of Ravan frightened to see this disturbance. Mandodari again tried to suggest Ravan for his deeds. She said, you please have faith on my words. He is omnipresent Brahma, that is God. You please consider this fact that the for vedas are the parts of his body. He is present in every particle of the world. So please leave enmity with him and go into the feet of Sri Ram and try to get his devotion which is a pleasure. He laughed to hear the advise of the woman. He remarked the nature of the women. Ravan said :

अवगुन आठ सदा उर रहहीं।
नारि स्वभाव सत्य कब कहहीं॥
Aavagun aath sada ur rahahin.
Naari swabhav satya kab kahahin.
साहस, अनृत, चपलता, माया, भय, अविवेक, असौच अदाया॥
Sahas, anrut, chapalta, maya, bhay, avivek, asoch adaya.

He told that this is the nature of women that they never speak truth. Eight types of evils are always present in them. By nature the women are courageous, liar, active and notorious, posing towards attraction, fearsome, dull minded, unpious and unkind. Thus, you have praised the virtues of the enemy and frightened me. I know it well that in this way you are praising me in an indirect way now Mandodari thought within herself that her husband is going in the lap of death. So no one could check him due to his mental disturbance. Now the whole demon generation will go ruin.

On the other hand Sri Ram awakened in the morning and called his courtiers to think over the problem. Jamwant bowed his head low and said, Sir you are almighty no doubt but as far as I think, Angad the son of Bali should go there once more as an ambassador to advise Ravan. Everyone was convinced to this proposal. Thus, Sri Ram asked Angad to go to Lanka to convince him that war will be harmful for him. So if he accepts his mistakes and gives back Sita with honour, then there is no question of war. Obeying his Lord, Angad bowed low and marched towards Lanka alone. As he entered the city, the son of Ravan who was playing on the way met to Angad. Both were young and powerful. In between the talks they began to fight with each other. He tried to kick Angad, but Angad caught his leg and threw him on the ground. He died. All the demons who saw this scene were frightened enough that they could speak nothing. There was a hue and cry in Lanka that the same monkey has come again who had burnt Lanka before some time. In this way, he reached at the gate of the court of Ravan without any hesitation taking the image of Sri Ram in his heart. Through an ambassador Ravan called him in his court. When Angad entered the court he saw that Ravan was sitting on the throne like black mountain. His mouth and nose appeared like the cave of the hills. His hair seemed like the trees on the mountains. When he entered the court all of his courtiers raised from their seat in his nonour. Ravan became very angry at this behaviour of his courtiers. It was his bravery that he entered in the court in the same way as a lion enters the gathering of elephants without any fear, because the mercy of Sri Ram was always with him.

A discussion started between Angad and Ravan. Ravan asked, who are you monkey? He said, I am the ambassador of Sri Ram You had been the friend of my father. So thinking for the welfare of your family, I have come to convince you and advise you that you are born in a high level family. After a hard penance you have gotten the blessings of Lord Shiva through which now you are the emperor of the world. And due to proudness you have kidnapped Mother Sita. She is not only my mother but she is the mother of the world. She is your mother also. Now you please consider my request. Take a loaf of grass in your mouth and with all of your queens go into the feet of Sri Ram and give back Sita with honour. When he will see you in this position, he will excuse you because he is very kind hearted. At this Ravan became very angry and warned Angad not to speak like wise. Angad said, Shiva and Brahma are always willingly ready to serve the feet of sri Ram, so he is not an ordinary man. He is superhuman. In this way for the welfare of your family you please go in his feet. Ravan said to Angad that there is no rival of me in your army. Your Lord and his younger brother both have become lean and thin due to starvation. My younger brother is sufficient for you and Sugreeva. Jamwant the minister has become so old. Nal-Neel are the only building maker they are the best sculptures, no doubt but they can not fight in the battlefield. The monkeys and bears are our food. There is only one scort in your army. Who has come here at first and burnt the city. Angad was wonder-struck to hear this, and asked again that in fact he has burnt your city? No body had faith that a small scale monkey may burn the city of Ravan. He was the runner of Sugreeva whom you have praised so much. He may go very fast but actually he may not be brave.

In fact love and war is done with persons of the same status. Actually you cannot win with my simple soldier. If a great man kills a frog, no one would praise him. In the same way if our Lord Sri Ram kills you it will be against his personality and dignity. Ravan laughed at this and said, well monkey, it is your nature to fulfil the wish of your master. Angad asked Ravan please tell me, how many Ravans are there in the world? As far as my knowledge is concerned and whatever I have heard I shall tell you. There was one Ravan who went to win Bali the king of Patal Puri, but bali who had gone to take bath daily in the seven oceans and then he take bath in the ocean. He went on the shore. He saw that Bali is standing in the mid of the ocean. he was worshipping God Sun. Ravan silently entered in the ocean and tried to kill him in water. But by nature the monkeys are clever. So he understood that someone is coming towards him. He got ready. As Ravan caught him from behind, he again took him in his arms and jumped from ocean to ocean. When he came back home after taking bath, he tied the Ravan at that place where horses were kept. There was another Ravan who had thousands of arms. He used to run on the earth like a special type of creature. To whom also Bali took to his house. But Rishi Pulasti went there and requested to leave him. The third Ravan is sitting before me. Thus, who are you among these Ravan? Ravan replied angrily, listen, I am that Ravan who used to play with the mountain Kailash like a ball in his hands. I have cut my heads many times to worship Lord Shiva. If an elephant rides on a boat and then it begins to move here and there in the same way when I walk on the ground, it begins to move. Thus, you are taking me lightly and praising the man. Well monkey, now I have came to know that how much knowledge you have? Now Angad couldn't check his anger.

जब तेहि कीन्ह राम कर निन्दा।
क्रोधवंत अति भयउ कपिन्दा॥
कटकटान कपि क्रुंजर भारी।
दोउ भुज दण्ड तमकि महिमारी॥

Jab tehi kinh Ram kar ninda.
Krodhvant ati bhayau kapinda.
Katkataan kapi krunjar bhari.
Dou bhuj dand tamaki mahimari.

He asked Ravan not to speak like this. Listen Ravan! the monkey, who had killed your son with all of his army, ruined your garden, how you can say that he is an ordinary monkey. In this way leave your all type of cleverness and remember Sri Raghunath. If You are a stupid fellow trying to maintain the enmity with Sri Ram, even then Brahma and Shiva also could not save you. So play with your heads like ball. When Sri Ram will become angry in the battlefield and He will shoot the arrows on you, then your boasting will go down. Hearing such type of words Ravan burst with anger and said, I have brother Kumbhakarna and son Sakrari, who are invincible. You have not listened to something about my bravery. I have won all the creatures of the world. Nobody can dare to stand before me.

At last Angad told Ravan that I have not come here as an ambassador. Sri Ram has send me to tell you again that if an elephant kills the jackal, there is no dignity in it by doing it. Otherwise I am all alone sufficient enough to take Sita from here. I can break your jaws. I fear of Sri Ram, otherwise, I can crush you and your supporters. I can take Sita with all your queens to Sri Ram. Again he preached Ravan and said, if I will do so no one will appreciate me, because to kill the dead person is no way to get fame. In proof he put the example that fourteen creatures are like living dead. As who promises and does nothing, the lustful person, the miser, the stupid fellow, so poor, defame person, so old with wrinkles on the face, always live like a patient, permanently angry, anti God and anti religion and saints. He who works for their own stomach, he who opposes everyone, is the great sinner. Thinking this I am not going to kill you. Please do not compel me to become angry. When again Ravan insulted Sri Ram the anger of Angad increased at high level. He roared like a lion and thumped his hands on the ground. In this way the earth began to tremble, the earth moved and

Ravan fell sown from his throne and somehow he controlled himself. But his crowns fell down on the ground. Ravan took some of them and arranged them on his heads. But Angad took four of them and threw it towards the camp of Sri Ram.

When the monkeys saw that some shining thing is falling in the army campus, they began to run here and there. Lord Sri Ram laughed and said, these are the crowns of demon King Ravan, which are being thrown by Angad from Lanka. Hanuman, at once, jumped and caught them. He put it before Sri Ram. It was shining like sun in the day also.

On the other hand Ravan said angrily to his soldiers to kill the monkey. Again the prince of Bali said, you the shameless fellow! Even now you are again boasting. I think you are suffering from mental disturbance. So you are murmuring like a crack man. You will get its result very soon. Yet, you are thinking about Ram that, He is an ordinary man.

Angad put a condition before Ravan by his own side. He challenged with anger that if any one of you can move my leg for even a single inch, I can go back leaving Sita here. I shall accept my defeat, Sri Ram also will go back. Everyone of his courtiers tried their best but they all failed. Then Ravan himself got up and as he bowed towards the leg of Angad, he requested Ravan not to touch his legs. But he should go and touch the feet of Sri Ram. Ravan was much ashamed with this event.

In the evening, Ravan went home sadly. Mandodari again tried to convience Ravan to leave enmity with Sri Ram. She said, you think yourself to be very brave but you could not cross the little line drawn by Laxman. My honourable husband, whom you want to win in the war, whose ambassador had done this. He crossed the sea in a jump. He ruined our gardens and before your eyes he killed Akshay Kumar. He had no fear at all with you. When he was burning the town where was your power please consider for my request again. Now give up boasting and go in the feet of Sri Ram. Never consider him in ordinary sense. He is the creator and destructor of the whole world. Mareech your maternal uncle knew well the effect of his arrow. You think, in the Swayambar of Sita in Janakpur there were thousands of kings in that gathering and you were also present there. There Sri Ram had broken the bow and married Sita. You should take Sita by force from there. Where was your power at that time. The son of Indra tried to take a test of His power and so He left his life on mercy and made him one eye blind. Even your sister, Surpnakha, was punished by him. Even then you did not feel the shame. He killed the demons like Biradh, Khar-Dushan, Kabandh with a little effort. He killed the giant Bali in only one stroke of his arrow. Thus, when you see these supreme activities in Him, then why you do not have faith in him as God. He made the bridge over the surface of water on the ocean. Again thinking for your welfare he send ambassador to convince you. In the midst of your court he challenged you like a lion, but you could do nothing of him. He has the followers like Hanuman and Angad who are bravest of the brave. Whom you say Human again and again. The person whose death is so near, he talks and behaves like you. The teaching of Mandodari were pinching him like needle.

Early in the morning Ravan went to his court. He sat on the throne with proud and forgot all the troubles through which he was surrounded. Here, Sri Ram called Angad near to him. Sri Ram said that I feel much curiosity to know that how have you found the crown of Ravan? Because he is the most powerful creature. Angad replied gently, they were not the crown but they were four virtues of a king. Consolation, wealth, punishment and separation all these four types of virtues always live in the heart of the kings. The Vedas tell us clearly about this. On getting Ravan without principle, they have come to you. They found that Ravan is against religion and against your devotion, so these virtues have come in your feet. Sri Ram smiled at his talkative nature. And then Angad told him all about Lanka and What had happened there. When Sri Ram came to know all about the strength of demons He called of his courtiers to him. He said there are four main big gates in Lanka. How we should arrange our army there? After discussion between Sugreeva, Jamwant and Vibhishan, they came to conclusion to prepare four division of the army. They deputed their commanders according to need. All the commanders were warned about their actions and duties.

They roared remembering Ram and Laxman. The whole Lanka was surrounded by the monkeys and bears. They were making sound from their mouth.

घटाठोप करि चहुँ दिसि घेरी।
मुखहिं निसान बजावहिं भेरी॥

Ghatatop kari chahun disi gheri.
Mukhahin nissan bajavahin bheri.

There was a great hue and cry in Lanka. People were afraid to see it. When Ravan knew this fact, he laughed with proudness at the deeds of the monkeys. He ordered his armies to defend Lanka by all means. A fierce battle took place between the two armies. The military drum, were beaten by the both sides, hearing that the soldiers felt pleasure. On one hand in the army of Ram the soldiers were saying Ram Chandra ki jai, and on the other hand in the army of Ravan the soldiers were saying Ravan ki jai. After some time the monkeys rushed and crushed the demon army and they began to run away from the battlefield as the clouds flew with the arrival of the storm.

In Lanka people were weeping and crying. The women and children were crying and abusing Ravan because he had offered death.

सब मिलि देहि रावनहिं गारिं।
राज करत यहि मृत्यु हंकारी॥

Sab mili dehi. Ravanhin gari
Raj karat yahi mrutyu hankari

When he saw that his army is going back, he asked everyone not to leave battlefield, otherwise they may be killed.

सर्वसु खाइ भोग करि नाना।
समर भूमि भये बल्लभ प्राना॥

Sarvasu khai bhog kari nana
Samar bhumi bhaye ballabh prana.

Due to fear of Ravan his army returned back and began to fight with the double courage. The demons threw several type of weapons on the monkeys. Now the monkeys were running back due to fear. But the fact is this that they will win the battle after all when Hanuman heard that his army is in trouble, he roared like a lion. Now Angad and Hanuman were fighting angrily. They ran on the palace of Ravan and began to break its tombs into pieces. The women and demons were crying in the fear to see the same monkeys in such a huge body. After killing the whole army of the demons, they came back to Sri Ram. Sri Ram touched the heads of all the soldiers. Thus, they lost their exertion and became fresh.

On the next day, both of the armies met in the battle field. Now the demon commanders Anip, Akampan, Atikaya were fighting bravely. The army of the monkeys and bears were also fighting bravely. Thus, in the day time it became dark in the battlefield with the dust. It seemed that the blood is raining from the sky. It was a dense dark in the battlefield. In this way no one could see each other and the monkeys became worried with this event. They were crying there and calling to each other. Lord Sri Ram knew all the secret of this darkness. So he called Agad and Hanuman gave them a little guidance about that. They ran angrily towards the demon army. Then Sri Ram shot an arrow of fire, by which a flash of light came there. Thus, the whole darkness of the battlefield was turned into light. Now the whole monkeys rushed on the demon army. When Angad and Hanuman roared in the battlefield the demon army began to run away. The monkeys caught them and threw them in the ocean. The creatures of the ocean began to eat them. Thus, the whole demon army was crushed by the monkeys. When the four armies saw that it is going to be dark of night, they all came back to their camps. Then Sri Ram saw them with kind eyes and they all lost their tireness.

राम कृपा करि चितवा सबही।
भये विगतश्रम वानर तबहीं॥

Ram kripa kari chitwa sabahi.
Bhaye Vigatshram vanar tabahin

On the other hand Ravan called his courtiers for conversation. He said, half of the army has been killed by the monkeys. Now what should be done.

आधा कटकु कपिन्ह संधरा।
कहहु वेगि का करिय विचारा॥

Aadha kataku kapinha sandhara.
Kahahu vegi ka kariya vichera

There was an old demon who had been once the minister of the parents of Ravan. He told Ravan that since when you have stolen Sita, I use to see bad dreams. I think it is not good for you and your family also. Sri Ram whom Vedas and Puran are praising, and whoever have gone against him, he had to suffer a lot. Mallyawant further said that he had killed Hirannyakchh and Madhukaitabh the bravest of the brave with a little effort. So he is not a simple man. He is super man that is God. Even Lord Shiva and Brahma are worshipping him continuously, then how you can oppose him. So please give back Sita to Ram. Hearing his suggestion Ravan got angry and called him names. He ordered him to leave the court at once.

Now Gannad the son of Ravan requested his father and said, that you need not worry my honourable father, I shall give him a great defeat. Thus, Ravan got a little satisfaction. He got seated his son on his lap and praised his fearlessness. Thinking and discussion in such a way the night passed. Early in the morning the monkeys gathered on four gates of Lanka again. There was a great hue and cry in whole Lanka. The demons ran towards the monkeys taking different types of weapons in their hands. Fact is this that the monkeys were bare handed. So they also began to throw heavy stones on the fort. The monkeys were also very clever and powerful so they caught the same stones and threw it on the fort. In this way maximum demons were injured with stones. When Meghnad came to know that all of his army is injured, he opened the door of the fort and marched ahead alone towards the battlefield. He called by name to Ram-Laxman, Nal-Neel, Dubid, Sugreeva, Angad and Hanuman. He challenged Vibhishan also to come once before him in the battlefield. He said angrily that today I shall kill you all. Nobody could save you all. Saying this he left his arrow of snakes. The whole army of the monkeys began to run here and there. Everyone was trying to save his life. There was no monkey and bear in the battlefield who was without hurt. Everyone was so much injured that they were about to die. He shot ten arrows on every soldier of Ramadal. All the brave monkeys were fainted and laid down on the ground. Now Meghnad roared in the battlefield like a lion. Perhaps he would have thought that he had won the battle.

When Hanuman saw that his whole army has been injured by Meghnad he rushed on him like death himself. Hanuman took a heavy stone and angrily threw it on Meghnad. He ran in to the air but his chariot with all of his horses was ruined. Hanuman called him again but he did not appear in the battlefield because he knew about the super power and strength of Hanuman. After some time he went near Sri Ram and began to shoot arrows and different types of weapon on him. But Sri Ram cut all his weapons with a little effort. Seeing this he was much ashamed on himself. Now Laxman could not check himself. He bowed his head in the feet of Sri Ram and took his bow with anger. Hanuman and Angad also accompanied him with a huge army. When Ravan came to know this, he also sent a huge army in support of Meghnad. Again a fierce battle took place. The soldiers of both sides met according to their pair. Everyone was willing for their victory. There was a surprising sound in the battle from the sky. Sometime they became happy and sometime they became sad. Here, Goswami Tulsidas means to say that when Ramadal gets victory they become happy and when the demons were succeeding they became sad.

Now Laxman and Meghnad the two bravest of the brave are fighting each other. Laxman injured him badly. The son of Ravan thought within himself that, this fellow would kill me, so he took Virghatinin Astra in his hand and shot it on the breast of Laxman.

It gave a heavy jerk to Laxman he fainted and fell down in the battlefield. Meghnad tried to take away the body of Laxman but he could not lift if from the ground. He was ashamed and went away. In the meantime Hanuman came there. He took Laxman on his shoulders and presented before Sri Ram in a faint position. Sri Ram felt very sad to see his younger brother in such a position. Jamwant was also there. He suggested Sri Ram that there is a Vaidya in Lanka named Sushena. Only he can bring back his life. Hanuman got ready to bring him. He went to Lanka and brought him with the whole of his house. Sushena was thanking his fate to see his Ram. He bowed his head in the feet of Sri Ram and asked Hanuman to bring the medicine the Sanjeevani Booti from Dronagiri Mountain. He guided Hanuman that how he will get this Booti at the mountain. He told that the plant on which there would be natural light, that would be Sanjeevani Booti. Thus, taking proper guidance and bowing his head in the feet of his Lord Sri Ram Anjani Putra started to bring the Sanjeevani Booti towards Dronagiri Mountain.

There in Lanka the ambassador told Ravan all about the treatment of Laxman. He became very sad to hear this. Now Ravan came at the home of Kalnami the master of illusion. He also advised Ravan to leave enmity with Sri Ram and to worship him because he is super human. He is creator and destructor of the world both. Ravan became angry at this. And he ordered Kalnami to follow him. Thus, Kalnami went in the way of Hanuman and tried to cheat him. Hanuman understood his aim and killed him by their tail. When Hanuman reached at the mountain Dronagiri, he found that all the plants were providing light. Now he felt great purplexion. All of a sudden an idea came in his mind. He lifted the whole mountain on his palm and flew towards Lanka. On the way when he was passing over Ayodhya. Bharat saw him. Bharat thought of him to be a demon, he shot without pointed arrow and Hanuman fell down on the ground saying Ram Ram. When Bharat heard this voice Ram, Ram from the mouth of Hanuman, he thought him to be a devotee of Lord Sri Ram. He took Hanuman in his arms and tried to wake him.

Though Hanuman was badly hurt so he was not opening his eyes being faint. Bharat felt very sad and remembered Sri Ram in his heart to help him. The result was this that Hanuman woke up saying Ram, Ram. Bharat embraced him and became very happy and asked the welfare of Sri Ram, Laxman and Sita. Hanuman told him all about the accident of Laxman. He told him that Ravan has stolen Sita. Bharat was worried much to this news. He asked Hanuman to sit on his arrow by which he might be sent to his destination very soon. But Hanuman refused to do so, because he was confident about his fast service.

Hanuman requested Bharat to let him see all the mothers. He did the same. Hanuman entered in the palace of Ayodhya. He met all the mothers as a son. He was wonder-struck to see Urmila in a complete make-up. He asked her, that well mother Urmila when you know that your husband honourable Laxman is in such a miserable condition, yet you are not sad. Inspite of sadness you seem happy. What is the secret behind this? Urmila replied - you don't know Hanuman, come with me and see here in bangle a mirror is fitted. In which I see my husband very well from here. And at the time of departure from Ayodhya my husband had burnt a lamp. That lamp indicates the ups and downs of his life. If its flame will go dim, it means he is in some critical position and if its flame will raise high, it means he is in happiness. I see that the flame of this lamp grows higher and higher so no question arise of any casualty. In this way I feel pleasure. Every Indian lady feels pleasure on the arrival of their husband. Now Hanuman thought within himself that I have done so late. So he bowed his head in the feet of all the mothers and started hurriedly towards Lanka, where everyone of Ramadal was waiting for him impatiently.

When Sri Ram saw the miserable condition of their younger brother Laxman, he spoke like a common man. He said, half of the night has passed and yet our Hanuman has not come. He took Laxman in his lap who was in unconscious condition and began to praise his good deeds. These lines of Manas are indicating the sadness of Sri Ram:

अर्द्ध राति गई कपि नहि आयउ, राम उठाइ अनुज उर लायउ।
सकहु न दुखित देखि मोहि काउ, बन्धु सदा तब मृदुल सुभाउ॥
Ardha raati gayi kapi nahi aayau, Ram uthai anuj ur layau.
Sakahu Na Dukhit dikhi mohi kau, bandh sada tar mridul subhau.

Tears appeared in the eyes of Sri Ram and he wept bitterly. When the monkeys heard the sound of their Lord Sri Ram, they became so sad. Their heart was filled with grief. In the meantime at the dawn of night Hanuman reached there with medicine, the Sanjeevani Booti. Ram took him in his arms with joy. His heart filled with gratitude towards Hanuman. At once, Vaidya Sushena arranged the medicine. As he gave the Booti to Sri Lakhanji he woke up. Lord Sri Ram met him and embraced him. There was joy and pleasure in the whole army. Hanuman sent back Vaidya Sushena to his residence. When Ravan, came to know about the fitness and good health of Laxman, he became very sad. He went to his younger brother Kumbhakaran who was sleeping from a long time. He awakened him. When he woke up he asked the reason of his sadness, Ravan told him all about the situation. He told Kumbhakaran how he had kidnapped Sita, the wife of Sri Ram. He further told that most of his commanders have died in the battlefield. Hearing the words of Ravan, Kumbhakaran felt very sad and remarked you are willing of your goodness stealing Sita, the mother of the hole world. He said, why have you awakened me? O Ravan! You have not done good. Even now, you have lost nothing. Please set aside your proud and go into the feet of Sri Ram. Sri Ram is not an ordinary man. He is super human. If you would had told me before, I may have suggested you, whatever Rishi Narad had told me. But the time has passed. He remembered Sri Ram for a while within himself and felt pleasure hearty.

Now Ravan arranged him for some vegetarian eatables. He ate them up and drank a lot of wine. Thus, he roared loudly like the thunder of the cloud. Leaving aside all of their army, he marched alone towards the army of Sri Ram because he thought himself to be the bravest of brave.

कुम्भकरन रन रंग विरूद्धा, सन्मुख चला काल जन क्रुद्धा।
Kumbhkaran run rang virudha, sanmukh chala kaal jan kruda.

When Vibhishan saw Kumbhakaran coming towards the battlefield, he came forward and touched his feet. Vibhishan told Kumbhakaran all about the behaviour of Ravan that he had kicked him on his good advise. Kumbhakaran embraced his brother and appreciated him for his good deeds. He thanked him that he had become the devotee of Sri Ram. Kumbhakaran thanked him again and said that he had become the shining star of his family by going in the feet of Sri Ram. He further expressed his idea that now I shall not go back home because I have to fight against Sri Ram to get moksha. Thus, Vibhishan came back to Sri Ram and told him about the reaching of

Kumbhakaran in the battlefield. Hearing this the monkeys ran towards the battlefield. They rooted out heavy trees and stones in their hands and began to throw it on Kumbhakaran. But he felt no harm from these things. He stood firm in the battlefield like a mad elephant. Then Kumbhakaran rushed on the monkeys and began to crush them by his hands and legs. All the army of Sri Ram was crushed by him. Even Angad, Hanuman and Sugreeva also fainted in the battlefield.

Now Kumbhakaran ran towards Sri Ram. When Sri Ram saw him coming towards him, he took his bow in his hand and began to shoot the arrows on him. It seemed that the arrows are raining on him in thousands of numbers. The arrows were cutting the body of the demons into pieces. The demons began to fell in the battlefield. Within a few minutes the hole demon army was ruined. When Kumbhakaran saw their army was finished. He became more angry and roared like a lion. He took a piece of rock of the mountain in his hands and began to throw it on the monkeys he began to crush the armies of Sri Ram by his legs as the mad elephant crushes the lotus flowers. The monkeys were crying and calling their Lord Sri Ram. When Ram heard the cry of his army, he left aside his army and rushed on Kumbhakaran alone. He shot the arrow on him and cut his heavy body into several pieces. When he fell on the ground the earth began to tremble. The light of his body entered in the heart of Sri Ram. Every body was wonder-struck to see this. Even the gods were also in wonder to see it. The gods were overjoyed at this happening . They were playing their flute and showering flowers from the sky. Here our honourable and world famous poet Goswami Tulsidas says that no one could describe the beautious scene of Sri Ram.

निश्चिर अघम मलाकर ताहि दीन निज धाम।
गिरिजा ते नर मंदमति, जे न भजहिं श्री राम॥

Nishichar agham malakar tahi deen nij dhaam.
Girija te nar mandmati, je na bhajahin Sri Ram.

Lord Shiva says to Parwati that the persons who don't remember Sri Ram are dull minded and unlucky, because he is so kind that he gave moksha and sent to heaven to the demons also, who have been evil doors for the whole life. At sunset both the armies came back to their camps. Sri Ram saw them with the kind eyes and thus they regained their energy and became fresh. But on the other hand the demons were going to be finished day by day.

छीजहिं निसिचर दिन अरूराती।
निज मुख सुकृत कहे जेहि भाँती॥

Chhijahin nisichar din arurati,
Nija mukh sukrit kahe jehi bhanti.

When Ravan heard about the death of his brother Kumbhakaran, he felt grief and wept bitterly. At the same time Meghnad came there and pacified his father. He said that I have achieved a special power from my honourable family God, which I have not shown you. I shall show you my doings in the battlefield tomorrow. Between this conversation the night passed and they found that the monkeys have covered the whole Lanka specially at the four main gates. Both the armies met in the battlefield. The demons were so brave and the monkeys were the bravest of brave. In the meantime, Meghnad, rode on his chariot and went in the sky. Then he roared from there. Thus, the monkeys were frightened on his behaviour. He began to throw different type of weapons from the sky like arrows, swords and stones. There was weapons everywhere in the battlefield. A fearful sound was filled in the whole atmosphere. But nobody could understand this at all that who is doing all this. Angad, Nal-Neel, Hanuman, Sugreeva and even Laxman were also fainted by him. Now he went to Sri Ram and began to fight with him. He shot the snake arrow on him. Thus, snakes tied the body of Sri Ram by all sides. In this way the supreme power which is untouched from worldly pleasure and pains, let tie their body in the battlefield. In this connection Parvatiji says that on remembering whom, the Rishi and Muni cut the Bhaw Bandhan it is his game that he himself is tied with Nagpash. Thus, persons who are actually wise they worship and pray Sri Ram leaving all the things aside.

गिरिजा जासु नाम जपि, नर काटहिं भव पासा।
सोकि बंध तर आवइ, व्यापक ब्रह्ममनिवासा॥

Girija jasu, naam japi, nar katahin bhav paas,
Soki Bandh tar aavai, vyapak Brahmaniwas.

When Meghnad saw the whole army in such a miserable condition, he came in his original form and began to abuse Sri Ram in the battlefield. When Jamwant saw him doing like this, he challenged him and rushed at him with full swim. He injured Meghnad badly by his own sphere. Thus, Meghnad became senseless, he caught him by his legs and threw him upon Lanka. He fell before Ravan in unconscious situation.

मेघनाद कै मुरछा जागी, पितहि बिलोकि लाज अति लागी।
Meghnad key murcha jagi, pitahi biloki laaj ati laagi.

When he came in his consciousness, and saw his father before him, he was much ashamed. He decided to go to forest for penance. On the other hand, Vibhishan told Sri Ram all about Meghnad, he said that if Meghnad will succeed in his penance, he would become immortal. Now it is necessary to ruin his devotion and to disturb his penance. Sri Ram suggested Laxman, Angad and Hanuman to go to Meghnad and ruin his penance. They bowed their hands and went to Meghnad. They disturbed his penance and so being angry he rushed on them with his sphere. Again he crushed all of them and stood before Sri Ram. As Sri Ram shot him with his arrow he flew away in the sky. Now Laxman became so angry and remembering Sri Ram he shot his arrow which entered in the mid of his chest. Meghnad fell down on the earth. And at the time of his death, he left all his delusion and said Ram! Ram! At this everyone thanked his fate. Now Hanuman took his dead body gently and put it at the main gate of Lanka. All the gods and gandharvas became very pleased to see his death. They showered flowers from the sky, played flutes and praised to Sri Ram again.

When Ravan came to know this fact that today his dearest and bravest son Meghnad also had been killed, he sank into grief. he fainted in the palace. Mandodari his mother wept for his bravery. All the countrymen of Lanka were also very sad at his death and every body was abusing Ravan for his bad deeds. Thus, Ravan pacified everyone and told that this very body is mortal. He told that every worldly creature is mortal. No one is immortal. So there is nothing to bother about deads.

पर उपदेश कुसल बहुतेरे।
जे आचरहिं ते नर न घनेरे॥
Par updesh kusal bahutere
Je aacharahin te nar na ghanere.

On the other day Ravan called his army commanders and said, those who want to run away from the battlefield, they may go willingly, because I have challenged the enemy on behalf of my own courage. Saying this he ordered to prepare his superfine chariot and asked to beat the military drum. His whole army marched towards the battlefield as the black storm. When the army marched with all of his strength, the earth began to move. The soldiers were roaring like a lion. He determinded to kill the two brothers. He was proud of his power.

As the monkeys knew this news that Ravan himself is coming with a huge army in the battlefield, they also rushed on his army like a storm. Both armies met in the battlefield and they began to fight each other. In the battlefield there was a contradiction. Ravan was on the chariot where Sri Ram were on foot. Seeing this Vibhishan became very much worried.

**रावन रथी विरथ रघुवीरा, देखि विभीषन भयउ अधीरा।
अधिक प्रीति मन मा संदेहा, बंदि चरन कह सहित सनेहा॥**

Ravan rathi virath Raghuvira, dekhi Vibhishan bhayau adhira.
Adhik priti man ma sandeha, bandi charan kah sahit sneha.

He said to Sri Ram gently, Well Lord! You are barefooted and you have no chariot. Then how would you win the powerful enemy. Sri Ram replied at this and said, well dear friend listen, the chariot of victory should be like this, on which the wheels are madeup of bravery and patience. Whose flag is madeup of truth and gentleness. Whose horses are madeup of strength and wisdom and those horses are fastened in the rope of excuse, mercy and equality. To worship to feet of Guru and Brahma is a bullet proof jacket for the rider on the chariot. This is the best and invincible chariot to win the enemy. This religious chariot will become invincible in the whole world. When Vibhishan heard the description of a winning chariot he was much influenced and touched the feet of Sri Ram. In this way he became sure about the victory of Sri Ram.

Now the war started between the both enemies. Goswami Tulsidas describes here very minutely that all the gods were seeing this war from the sky, even Lord Shiva was present there to see the interesting war. The monkeys were cutting, crushing, beating, rushing and fighting the demon armies. In response the demons were also throwing different type of weapons on them. Thus, a fierce battle took place between the two armies. The river of blood began to flow in the battlefield. The dead bodies were floated in the river. The eagles were eating for the flesh of dead bodies and crying wildly. Actually there was a fearful scene in the battlefield. There was too much blood shed in that war. In this way the demon army appeared on the run away. When Ravan saw that his armies was running away, he, at once, came forward and drove the chariot towards the monkey army. As soon as Ravan rushed on them and began to crush them from their body, the monkeys were frightened and began to run, here and there. They were calling Angad, Hanuman and even Sri Ram also for their help. When Laxman saw this scene, he challenged Ravan and remarked you stupid fellow, you are the thief, you are a nonsense, why are you killing monkeys and bears? Stop there. Look at me. I am standing before you like your death itself. Accepting his challenge Ravan said, you the killer of my son, I was searching for you. Today I shall take sigh of relief by killing you. Saying this he shot a most powerful arrow on Laxman, but he cut it into several pieces by his own arrow. Now Ravan used the Bramha Shakti on Laxman, and he fell fainted on the ground. Seeing this Hanuman rushed on Ravan and gave a heavy blow on his hand and on his face. The blow. was so powerful that Ravan bent down on his knees. He fainted for a while. When Ravan wokeup and came in sense he began to praise the power of Hanuman. But Hanuman replied, it is my unfortunate and it is shameful for me, that you are yet alive after facing my blow on your face. Saying this Hanuman took Laxman before Lord Sri Ram. When Ravan saw this scene he was wonder-struck to see the strength of the monkey. On the other hand, when Sri Ram touched and praised Laxman for his bravery, he awakened and got up. Again he started his battle in the same flow. Now the anger of Laxman was in peak. Thus, he ruined the chariot of Ravan fully and he had to run away from the battlefield. In this way Laxman came to Sri Ram and bowed his head in Ram's feet.

This is the peak of his foolishness that even now Ravan wishes for victory. And so he started a yagna against Sri Ram. When Vibhishan came to know this fact, he told all to Sri Ram and requested that if this duffer fellow will succeed in the yagna, he will become immortal. And then nobody could kill him. So it would be better that we should go there to disturb his yagna at any cost. On the other morning Hanuman, Angad and some other monkeys climbed on Lanka. They began to abuse Ravan badly. They caught the hair of his wives and they started crying. Now Ravan could not control himself. Thus, he rushed on the monkeys with his sphere. In this way his yagna was disturbed by the monkeys. All the monkeys came back to Sri Ram and told him the whole story of their destruction of yagna in Lanka. In this way Ravan left the hope of his life and marched with his army towards the battlefield. Now the gods requested Sri Ram to kill him very soon because he had pained them very much.

इहाँ देवन्तह अस्तुति कीन्ही, दारून विपति हमहिं यहि दीन्ही।
अब जनि राम खेलावहु यही, अतिसय दुखित होति बैदेही॥

Ihan Devantah astuti kinhi, darun vipati hamahin yahi dinhi.
Ab jani Ram khelavahu yehi, atisay dukhit hoti baidehi.

Hearing their kind request Sri Ram took the bow in his hands and got ready for war. Here Goswami Tulsidas very remarkably describes about the preparance of Sri Ram for war. When Sri Ram moved their hands on the bow, a fearful sound came out form the bow and the result was that all the creatures of the world were frightened and the elephants of ten direction began to cry. In this way the earth also began to move. The oceans and mountain also began to move.

In the meantime, the army of the enemy appeared coming towards the battlefield. The war started between the both armies. Sri Ram angrily shot arrows on the enemies in thousands of numbers. Thus, the demons were injured and they began to run away from the battlefield. There was a great blood shed. The river of blood began to flow in the battlefield. The ground was filled with the dead bodies of the demon soldiers. Now Ravan thought within himself that the whole demon army is about to finish. I am all alone and the monkeys and bears are several in numbers. So I should take help to illusion. The gods saw that our Lord is barefooted and on foot in the battlefield and Ravan is on chariot, So they sent to special chariot of Indra for Sri Ram. Sri Ram rode on the chariot. When the monkeys saw their Lord riding on the chariot they received encouragement and rushed on the enemy.

तेज पुंज रथ दिव्य अनुपा, हरषि चढ़े कोशल पुर भूपा।

Tej punj rath divya anupa, harashi chadhe kaushal pur bhoopa.

When the monkeys beated and crushed the demons badly, then Ravan expanded his illusion. There appeared a lot of Ram and Laxman in the battlefield. The monkeys were worried to see this scene. But Sri Ram understood the secret. And within no time he turned all the illusion into reality. The monkeys army became pleased at this. Now Ravan Came forward and stood before the chariot of Sri Ram. He dropped several weapons on him at a time but Sri Ram cut all of them by a little effort. Then he killed all the horses of the chariot of Sri Ram and even the driver also. Sri Ram made them alive by his Godly effect. And then he angrily shot his arrows on Ravan. First of all he ruined his chariot with all of his horses and shot a lot of arrows on

Ravan. He was much injured at this. Now Vibhishan the brother of Ravan told Sri Ram about the secret of his death. He told that there is nectar in the stomach of Ravan and due to this Ravan is immortal. So you please first of all shoot the arrow in the mid of his stomach only then he may be killed. in this way when Sri Ram came to know the secret of his death, he was much pleased. He shot thirty-one arrows at a time. One arrow struck in the mid of his stomach. Rest of the other arrows cut all of his heads in a stroke and then cut his body into several pieces. He fell down on the ground crying loudly. When his body fell down on the ground, the earth began to shake for a while and a lot of monkeys were crushed under his dead body. At the death of demon king Of Lanka, all the gods become much pleased. Not only the gods but all the worldly creatures felt a great pleasure at his death because everyone was much tortured by his bad deeds. There was pleasure in the army of Sri Ram. Everyone was praising the strength and supreme power of Sri Ram. They all were saying Siyavar Ram Chandra ki jai. The gods prayed Sri Ram again and again . The whole universe was filled with the sound of Jai Jai Jai. The gods were showering flowers from the sky. Lord Sri Ram looked at the gods with merciful eyes. They all became fearless. In this way Sri Ram has done his duty for which he had taken birth on the earth.

As soon as Mandodari heard about the death of her husband she fell fainted on the earth. All the queens were weeping and crying to see the miserable condition of their husband. Mandodari said, when you were alive, you had won all the kings of the world, even the gods also. Your sons and brothers were also so brave like you. Now this position is due of opposition of Lord Sri Ram.

राम विमुख अस हाल तुम्हारा।
रहा न कुल कोउ रोवन हारा॥
काल विवस पति कहा न माना।
अग जग नाथ मनुज करि जाना॥

अहइ नाथ रघुनाथ सम, कृपा सिन्धु नहि आन ।
जोगि वृंद दुर्लभ गति, तोहि दीन्ही भगवान॥

Ram vimukh asa haal tumhara.
raha na kul kou rovan hara.
Kaal vivas pati kaha na mana
Ag jag nath manuj kari Jana.
Aahaye nath Raghunath sama, Kripa Sindhu Nahi aan.

Jogi vrindh durlabh Gati, tohi dinhi baghwan.

Now the jackals will eat your heads as you have never trusted me because your time was finished. Well my Lord! there is no one so kind like Sri Ram, because he gave you the same status after death as he used to give his most lovable devotees. When Vibhishan saw the pitiable condition of Mandodari, he went to her and seeing the condition of his own brother he felt great sorry. Then Sri Ram sent Laxman to console Vibhishan and Mandodari. Thus, at the suggestion of Laxman they all paid there formal duties of funeral. After paying his formality for his dead body they took bath. Now Vibhishan came to Sri Ram and bowed low in their feet.

Sri Ram ordered Angad, Hanuman, Sugreeva and Laxman to go to Lanka with Vibhishan and arrange for the coronation of Vibhishan. He said that I am bound not to go to the city in concern to follow the order of my father. They did the same and arranged for the coronation of Vibhishan. They got seated Vibhishan on the throne and bowed low according to the custom. Now Vibhishan came to Sri Ram with them. Sri Ram showed his gratitude towards them. He said that now you have become the king of Lanka. And in coming days, the persons who will remember me with you, certainly they will get moksha and they will go across the bhawsagar without any effort. When the monkeys heard the sweet tone of Sri Ram they bowed low and laid down in their feet. Everyone was very pleased.

Lord Sri Ram asked Hanuman to go to Lanka to tell his News to Sita and you come soon to me with her welfare. Hanuman followed him and went there. The demon ladies showed him Sita from a distance. Hanuman touched the feet form a distance of mother Sita. He further told her all about the death of Ravan and about the victory of Lord Sri Ram. He also told that Sri Ram has made Vibhishan the king of Lanka. Now Janki became pleased at this news. Mother Sita will always reside in your heart. She further said that your good deeds will be remembered in the world for all the times to come. She asked Hanuman to tell Sri Ram to take her as soon as possible. Hanuman went to Sri Ram and told him the welfare of Sitaji. In this was he ordered Hanuman, Angad and Vibhishan to bring Sita. They went to Sita where the demon women were in her service. They dressed Sitaji well in complete make-up. Now they brought Sitaji to Sri Ram. Though Sitaji had been out from a long time, so Sri Ram called her names for a while. The demon ladies felt very sorry at this. But Sitaji did not oppose at this.

She spoke gently, If I am your devotee from body, mind and soul, my Lord, you can take my test as you like. Then Sri Ram asked laxman to arrange Chita fire for the test. Laxman did the same. He arranged some woods and Sitaji sat on that wood. He lit a fire. It begin to burn. Its flames were touching the sky. When Sitaji sat in the fire, she had remembered her Lord Sri Ram, so she could not be burnt. She was totally safe. Seeing this the gods began to shower flowers from the sky. Everyone was pleased with purity of Sita.

Thus, Sri Ram took a little test of Sitaji and became confident about her piousness. Now they sat on a stone with Sitaji. Seeing mother Sita with their Lord Sri Ram all the monkeys became so happy. They began to say Jai Raghunath, Jai Sri Ram. All the gods of the world appeared there at that time. They prayed Lord Sri Ram. Their heart was filled with gratitude. They all bowed their heads and said, O my Lord! Whenever we have felt trouble, only you have helped us taking several forms of the body. We had forgotten your devotion due to this we have suffered a lot. Now with your grace our all the difficulties have gone away. We are fearless now. So we are bowing our heads in your feet. They prayed for a long time to their Lord Sri Ram. The situation was this that they were not going to be satisfied with their prayer. They were looking the lotus eyes Prabhu SriRam. It is said that king Dashratha the father of Sri Ram came there. Tears of happiness appeared in his eyes, when he saw his son on this high rank. Sri Ram with Laxman touched the feet of their father Dashratha and then king Dashratha blessed them.

तेहि अवसर दसरथ तहँ आये।
तनय विलोकि नयन जल छाये॥
अनुज सहित प्रभु वन्दन कीन्हा।
आसिरवाद पिता तब दीन्हा॥

Tehi avasar Dasrath tahn aaye
Tanay viloki nayan jal chhaye
Anuj sahit prabhu vandan kinha
Aasirvad pita tab dinha.

Sri Ram said that by your grace we could win invincible demon king Ravan. Now Dashratha recognised his son that he is not an ordinary son. He is a supreme power the God himself. So Dashratha prayed again to Sri Ram and went to heaven. In this way the gods began to pray him again. They requested him to be merciful on them forever. Thinking of us as your devotee, be merciful on us and give us your devotion. Now the gods asked

Sri Ram about their further duties. Sri Ram said to Indra, to give life again to those bears and monkeys who were laying dead on the ground. These have been killed by the demons. All these have lost their lives for the sake of me. So you please Indra make them alive again. Now Indra poured nectar from the sky by the plane. The monkeys and bears woke up who were lying on the ground. But the demons remained lying there. They all were set free from Bhawa Bandhan. They went to heaven.

सुधा वृष्टि भइ दुहुँ दल ऊपर।
जिये भालु कपि नहिं रजनीचर॥
सुर अंसिक सब कपि अरू रीछा।
जिये सकल रघुपति की ईछा॥

Sudha vrishti bhai dvhun dal upar
Jiye bhalu kapi nahin rajnichar.
Sur ansik sab kapi aru richha.
Jiye sakal Raghupati ki ickcha.

The gods showered flowers on Sri Ram and prayed him as they could. Now they went away to their residence by their planes. Thinking it to be a good time Lord Shiva came to Sri Ram. Tears appeared in the eyes of Lord Shiva with love. He looked at his Lord. His heart was filled with gratitude. He began to pray Lord Sri Ram. He requested Lord Sri Ram to reside in his heart with Laxman and Sitaji. He further requested Sri Ram to let him allow to come Ayodhya at the time of his coronation and to see the Lord Again. When Shiva went away after prayer, then Vibhishan came to Sri Ram and surrendered all the property of Lanka in his feet. He asked Sri Ram to take little rest. But Sri Ram told Vibhishan, my dear brother, have become part and partial to each other. Thus, the fact is this, that your all the properties is mine. But when I think of Bharat, even a single minute for me passes like a thousands of years. I have given him a schedule time to reach Ayodhya. If I will not reach Ayodhya in due course of time, I will not find him alive. Thinking the condition of Bharat the heart of Lord Sri Ram filled with gratitude.

बीते अवधि जाउं जौ, जिपत न पावउँ वीर।
सुमिरत अनुज प्रीति प्रभु, पुनि पुनि पुलक सरीर॥

Bite avadhi jaun jo, jipat na pawaun vir.
Sumirat anuj priti prabhu, puni puni putak sarir.

He further blessed Vibhishan for a long and happy life. Sri

Ram blessed Vibhishan to get heaven in his last days, which the saints and sages get after their life.

Now Vibhishan went to Lanka. He filled the plane with several type of Jewels and precious clothes. He dropped it down among the army of Sri Ram from the sky. Goswami Tulsidas says that it is very difficult to see face to face Sri Ram for Rishies and Munies. But Sri Ram is enjoying between monkeys and bears. In this connection Lord Sri Ram is always fond of pious love not of penance and other type of prayer. When the monkeys got clothes and jewels, they dressed themselves in many colours. Sri Ram saw the monkeys in different type of dress, he laughed at them.

मुनि जेहि ध्यान न पावहिं, नेति नेति कह वेद।
कृपा सिन्धु सोइ कपिन्ह सन, करत अनेक विनोद॥

Muni jehi dhyan na pawahin, neti neti kah ved.
Kripa sindhu soi kapinh san, karat anek vinod.

He said gently, I have killed the Ravan by your support, I have made Vibhishan the king of Lanka. Thus, you have done your duty. Now you all please go your homes fearlessly. When the monkeys heard about their departure they became very sad. They said, we are belonging to the monkey race, and you are the father and creator of the whole universe. So we are ashamed of this how could we help you. The mosquito can never do any good of Garun the Lord of birds. All the monkeys and bears went away to their homes with the memory of Lord Sri Ram between the happiness and sorrow.

Angad, Nal-Neel, Jamwant, Sugreeva Vibhishan and the other commanders were standing like a statue to see the statement of Sri Ram. At once, he understood their love towards him. He took them on the pushpak Viman and bowed his head in the feet of Brahmans. Thus, he moved the viman in the north side. When the viman started, there was a great noise made by the viman and people began to say Siyavar Ram Chandra ki jai. There was a beautiful throne in the viman. Sri Ram and Sita sat on it. Pushpak viman started towards Ayodhya. The gods showered flowers on him. Now Sri Ram showed Sita the place where Indrajeet, Ravan and Kumbhakaran were killed in the battlefield. He also showed her Rameshwaram where he had established the image of Lord Shiva. Thus, Sita, Laxman and Sri Ram bowed their heads towards their Lord Shiva, wherever Sri Ram stayed in the forest during exile, he told Sita the names of those places with regard.

जहँ जहँ कृपासिन्धु वन, कीन्ह बास विश्राम।
सकल देखाये जानकिहिं, कहे सबन्हि के नामll
Jahn Jahn kripasindhu van, kinha baas vishram.
Sakal dekhaye jaankihi, kahe sabanhi ke naam.

Very soon Puspak viman reached Dandak forest. There they met Rishi Kumbhak also. They got blessing from all the saints and sages. They reached Chittrakoot also. From there they reached near Yamuna river. They worshipped Ganga river also. Now they reached Prayag, the king of the pilgrims. Ram said Sita to see Awadhpuri and to salute it. Ram also saluted Awadhpuri by heart now the Pushpak viman landed at Triveni. Now Sri Ram with all of their companions became fresh at Triveni. He donated the Brahmans. Lord Sri Ram asked Hanuman to go to Ayodhya in the form of Brahman to take care of Bharat. At once Hanumaji went to Bharat.

Now Lord Sri Ram went to Rishi Bharadwaj. The Rishi worshipped Sri Ram in different ways and prayed them by heart. He blessed Sri Ram also. When Nishadraj kewat came to know that Sri Ram has reached here, he made a great arrangement of boats to cross the pious river Ganga. The viman landed on the bank of river Ganga. There the mother Sita worshipped mother Sursari the Gagna. Mother Ganga blessed Sita for prosperous life.

तब सीता पूजी सुरसरी, बहुप्रकार पुनि चरनन्हि परी।
दीन्ह असीस हरषि मन गंगा, सुन्दरी तव अहिबात अभंगाll
Tab Sita puji sursari, bahu prakar puni charanhi pari.
Dinh asis harshi man Ganga, sundari tav ahibat abhanga.

Nishadraj came there and bowed down in the feet of Lord Sri Ram and mother Sita. Seeing this devotion in their feet, Sri Ram took him in his arms. Sri Ram got seated him by their side and asked welfare of him. Here, Goswami Tulsidas remarkably refers the dignity of Sri Ram that made great Kewat who had been at evil doors for the whole life. Sri Ram took him in his arms like his brother Bharat. So we should not forget our Lord Sri Ram in delusion. The character of Sri Ram should be remembered by all of us. If we would do so, it will be essential from all sides. Those persons who would hear the story of the victory of Lord Sri Ram and who would sing the victory story of Sri Ram, they will get victory in their life, they will get wisdom and power by the mercy of Lord Sri Ram. Goswami Tulsidasji says that this very Kaliyug is the centre of All evils. And by reasoning one can come to conclusion that there is no other base for us inspite of the name of Lord Sri Ram. Only the name of Sri Ram can take us across the Bhawasagar.

As far as our personal experience is concerned, I can say on the ground of Sri Ram Charit Manas that in this Kaliyug only Ram Nam is the base of life. The Ram Nam is Bhaw Tarak in this era. If we remember the name of Lord Sri Ram at the time of any difficulty, it is sure that the difficulty will go away. It will bring prosperity to our life.

यह कलिकाल मलायतन, मन करि देखु विचार।
श्री रघुनाथ नाम तजि, नाहिन आन अधार॥

Yeh kalikaal malayatan, man kari dekho vichar.
Shri Raghunath naam taji, nahin aan adhar.

Thus, Sri Ram Charit Manas ruins all the calamities of Kaliyug.

The Dignity of Lord Sri Ram

अमित रूप प्रगटे तेहि काला।
यथ योग मिले सबहि कृपाला॥
Amit roop pragate tehi kala,
Yatha yog mile sabrhi kripala.

Sri Ram appeared in the several forms and met with all his well wishers in a very short time.

Chapter 7
UTTAR KAND

All the mothers and the other well-wishers were gathering in the palace of Ayodhya and were thinking that the schedule time is going to be over and even then our Lord Sri Ram did not come back from the forest. So every citizen of Ayodhya was in perplex. Everybody was lean and thin in absence of Sri Ram. All of sudden they felt that, somebody is about to tell them that Sri Ram is reaching Ayodhya. The right hand and right eye of Bharat was vibrating and giing indication the arrival of Sri Ram with Laxman and Sita. All the mothers were pleased to see the good indication. Bharat was thinking that the time is going to be finished and even now our Lord Sri Ram has not come. What may be the reason? Perhaps, the thinks me a man of evil thoughts so he has forgotten me. Laxman had been the lucky one that he had followed him. He did not took me with him because he would have thought me as a cunning fellow. But the fact is that, he is very kind hearted, his nature is very simple, so it is my firm idea that he must come at his scheduled time. Being apart from Sri Ram, Bharat was thinking and becoming glad within himself at the same time, Hanumanji reached there in the form of a Brahman. He proved himself to be a ship for Bharat in ocean. Hanuman found that Bharat is sitting on the mat and his body has grown lean and thin in the shape of a saint. He is remembering Ram-Ram and tears are coming out from his eyes.

राम विरह सागर महँ भरत मगन मन होत।
विप्र रूप धरि पवन सुत, आइ गयउ जनु पोत॥

Ram virah sagar mahan Bharat magan man hot.
Vipra roop dhari Pawan soot, aayi gayau janu poth.

Now Hanuman spoke gently that whom you are remembering day and night, that very Lord Sri Ram is coming to Ayodhya with Laxman and Sita. He has won all the enemies and the gods are praising him.

जासु विरह सोचहु दिन रानी, रटहु निरन्तर गुन गन पाँती।
रघुकुल तिलक सुजन सुखदाता, आयउ कुशल देव मुनि त्राता॥
रिपु रन जीति सुजस सुरगावत, सीता अनुज सहित प्रभु आवत॥

Jaasu Virah sochahu din rati, ratahu nirantar gun gan pati.
Raghukul tilak sujan sukndata, aayau kushal dev muni tratha.
Ripu run jeeti sujas surugavath, Seeta anuj sahit Prabhu aavat.

When Bharat heard this sweet sound, he asked, who are you please and from where have you come gentleman? He told that I am the Hanuman, the follower of Sri Ram. Please listen to me. At once, Bharat stood up and took him in his arms happily with the tears in his eyes. Bharat said I have forgotten all the pains after seeing you. It seems that Lord Sri Ram has met me. Bharat requested Hanuman, please tell me all about Sri Ram in brief. Thus, Hanuman told him the whole story about Sri Ram in a short time. In this way Hanuman bowed low in the feet of Bharat and went back to Sri Ram. He told all about Bharat and Sri Ram rode on the Pushpak Viman and started towards Ayodhya.

Bharat came to Ayodhya from Nandi Village and he told all the news to Guru Vashishta. Again he went to the palace and told everyone about the arrival of their Lord Sri Ram. He told the welfare of Sri Ram to all the mothers also. Thus, when the citizens of Ayodhya came to know this fact, they ran to see their lovely Ram leaving all their necessary work aside. When Ayodhya came to know about the reaching of Lord Sri Ram, it was filled with the pleasures in itself. It became so charming. Thus, Bharat with the guru Vashishta, Brahmans and neighbours went happily to meet Lord Sri Ram on the way. They were waiting for their Ram impatiently.

On the other hand, Lord Sri Ram is showing to monkeys, the beautiful Ayodhya city. He told Hanuman, Angad and Vibhishan more about the pious city ayodhya. He said, though everyone praises the heaven for its goodness and even our Vedas also praise its dignity but it is not lovable for me in comparison to Ayodhya. Only kagbhushandi knew this secret thing. My birth place Ayodhya is very very pleasant for me.

जद्यपि सब बैकुण्ठ बखाना, वेद पुरान विदित जग जाना।
अवधपुरी सम प्रिय नहीं सोउ, यह प्रसंग जानइ कोउ कोउ॥
जन्मभूमि मम पुरी सुहावनि, उत्तर दिसि बह सरजू पावनि।
अति प्रिय मोहिं यहां के बासी, मम द्योमदा पुरी सुखरासी॥

Yadyapi sab beykunth bakhana, ved puran vidit jag jana.
Aawadpuri sam priya nahi sou, yeh prasang jaanaye kou kou.
Janmabhoomi mam puri suhavani. Nttar disi bah sarju pawani.
Ati priya mohi yahaan ke baasi, Mama dhyomada puri sukhrasi.

Its geographical situation is this, that pious river Saryu flows in its north side. He told them that the persons who take bath in this pious river they certainly go to heaven without any effort. Everybody was much pleased to hear the description. They thanked for the fate of Ayodhya, which was praised by Sri Ram himself. From the sky, when Sri Ram saw the gathering coming towards him, he motivated the Puspak Viman to land at Ayodhya. Though the Pushpak Viman had been out form a long period from its master Kuber, Lord Sri Ram motivated it to go to its master Kuber. And so it flew back happily to its master motivated by Sri Ram.

उतरि कहेउ प्रभु पुष्पकहि तुम्ह कुबेर पहिं जाहु।
प्रेरित राम चलेउ सो, हरषु विरहु अति ताहु॥
Uttari Kaheu prabhu pushpakahi tumh Kuber pahin jahu.
Prerit Ram chaleu so, harshu virahu ati tahu.

Sri Ram and the citizens of Ayodhya became very pleased. When Sri Ram saw that a great gathering wants to see their Lord, he played a wonderful role. He appeared in several own forms and met properly every one within no time.

अमित रूप प्रगटे तेहिकाला, यथा योग मिले सबहि कृपाला।
छन महं मिले सबहि भगवाना, उमा मरम यह काहु न जाना॥
Amit roop pragate tehikala, yatha yog mile sabahi kripala.
Chhan mahan mile sabahi Bhagwan, Uma maram yeh kahu na jaana.

Here Lord Shiva says to Uma that no one could understand this secret thing. Thus, by pleasing everbody, Sri Ram marched ahead towards the place to meet his all mothers.

All the mothers ran towards them as the cow mother runs towards her calve after having been out from a long period, which had gone to graze in the field.

कौसल्यादि मातु सब धाई। निरख बच्छ जनु धेनु लवाई॥
Kausalyadi maatu sab dhai, nirakh bach janu dhenu lawaii.

All the mothers met them happily but mother Kakeye met him with shame. Sita also met her mother-in-laws and touched their feet happily. They blessed her again and again for a prosperous and long life.

सासनहु सबनि मिली वैदेही, चरननि लागि हरषि अति तेहि।
देहि असीस बूझि कुसलाता, होहि अचल तुम्हार अहिबाता॥

Sasanhu sabni mili vaidehi, charanni lagi harshi ati tehi.
Dehi asis bujhi kuslata, hohi achal tumhar ahibata.

Mother Kaushalya looked at her sons again and again and thought within herself that my sons are so tender. How they have killed the powerful demon king Ravan? Sometime she sees Laxman and sometime Sita. She was overjoyed to see Sri Ram with Laxman and Sita before her.

Now Sri Ram asked his all the friends to touch the feet of his Guru Vashistha. He said that Guru Vashistha is honourable in my family. I have killed the mighty demons on behalf of his mercy and grace. By saying this he has raised high the place of Guru in our society. He moved towards the palace and the gods were showering flowers from the sky on them. Ayodhya was decorated in such a way that it seemed like a bridegroom. Our Nigam, Shesh and even mother Sharda the goddess of wisdom were describing the dignity of Ayodhya at that time. They were also wonder-struck to see the beautious scene of ayodhya then how the men could describe its dignity and beauty.

When Lord Sri Ram found that mother Kakeye is ashamed on behalf of her deeds so he first of all went to her home. He pacified her in many ways and then he entered in his home. Now Guru Vashistha ask the Brahmans and thinking it to be a good time, he requested them to throne Sri Ram very soon. They suggested him not to be late in such a good deed. Thus Guru Vashistha ordered Sumantra to arrange all the necessary things for the coronation of Sri Ram. Hearing this Sumantra arranged all the main necessities of coronation. Everything was prepared in a short time. First of all they decorated the whole Ayodhya as they could. All the friends of Sri Ram became fresh and took bath with the help of servants. Then Sri Ram with all of his brothers took bath, became fresh and dressed himself in princely dresses. The mother-in-laws arranged Sita for bath. They dressed her well in every respect.

In this way mother Sita sat in the left side of Sri Ram as the inn of beauty and virtue. Seeing this all the mothers became so happy and thanked their life.

राम बाम दिसि सोभति, रमा रूपा गुन खानि।
देखि मातु सब हरषी, जन्म सुफल निज जानि।
Ram ban disi sobhati, Rama roopa gun khani.
Dekhi matu sab harshi, janma sufal nij jaani.

Kagbhusandji says that at that time Brahma, Shiva and other gods came by their Vimans in the sky to see their Lord Sri Ram.

सुनु खगेस तेहि अवसर, ब्रह्मा सुर मुनि वृन्द।
चढि विमान आये सब, सुर देखन सुख कंद॥
Sunu khages tehi aavsar, Brahma sur muni vrind.
Chadi viman aaye sab, sur dekhan sukh kandh.

Now the Rishies asked for a grand throne. The throne was shining like the sun. Sri Ram sat on it bowing their head in the feet of the Brahmans. Sri Ram sat on the throne with Sitaji seeing this everyone became very glad. First of all Guru Vashistha made a red mark on the forehead of Lord Sri Ram. It was Raj Tilak. Then the other Brahmans also followed him. All the mothers were much pleased at that time and the gods played flutes from the sky when Lord Sri Ram sat on the throne. At that time Bharat with all the brothers and Angad, Hanuman and Vibhishan were busy into service of their elder brother Sri Ram. After praising their Lord, when all the gods went away then Vedas came there in disguise to worship and pray their Lord Sri Ram. Nobody could understand this secret except Lord Shiva. When Vedas went away Lord shiva came there and started praying and praising the good deeds of Sri Ram. Then Sri Ram arranged the proper residence for all the monkeys.

Lord Shiva says to kagbhusandi that the persons who listen this pious story of Lord Sri Ram they get relief from three type of troubles. Those troubles are physical, natural and spiritual. He further says that the persons who sing and recite the songs of Lord Sri Ram they get different types of wealth. They lead prosperous life and at last they go to heaven.

सुनु खगपति यह कथा पावनी, त्रिविध ताप भय दावनी।
जे सकाम नर सुनहि जे गावहि, सुख सम्पति नाना विधि पावहिं।
सुर दुर्लभ सुख करि जग माहीं, अंत काल रघुपति पुर जाहीं॥
Sunu khagpati yeh katha pawani, trividh tap bhay dawani.
Je sakaam nar sunahi je gawahi, sukh sampati nana vidhi pawahin.
Sur durlabh sukh kari jag mahi, anth kaal Rughupati pur jahin.

All the monkeys were living happily. They had a great devotion in the feet of Lord Sri Ram. So they forgot their homes. And in this way six months passed very easily. After some time, Lord Sri Ram called all his friends and said, you have served me a lot. How can I praise before or in front of you? You all have dedicated your homely pleasures due to me, so you are more lovable for me. He said that even my brothers, my kingdom, my wealth, my beloved Sita, my body, my palace, my family members and other relatives are not so lovable as you. You all are nearest and dearest for me. Thus he suggested all their friends to go to their homes and to remember him by heart. He also suggested them to realise this fact that I am omnipresent, I am almighty and I am the creator of all the worldly things. So your love towards me should be as it is. they all were much pleased to hear the words of Lord Sri Ram and they forgot that who and where they are. They were gazing their Lord. Due to great love, they could not speak even a single word. When Lord Sri Ram saw their great love towards them, he preached them about some spiritual knowledge. Now, Lord Sri Ram dressed them all in a good new dress and went to see off them. Angad, Nal-Neel, Jamwant, Sugreeva, Vibhishan, and Kewat all the main friends of Sri Ram went away towards their homes. They had seated the image of Lord Sri Ram in their hearts.

When Lord Sri Ram sat on the throne, all the creatures of world became very please. Everybody forgot all type of social differences with the grace of Lord Sri Ram. There was no enmity among the people. Not only men but the animals also forgot their enmity. The result was that, the lions and the cows were drinking water side by side. They were roaming in the forest together leaving their enmity aside. Everyone was following the rules and guiding lines of Vedas and Upnishads. And thus they were leading a prosperous life pleasantly without any fear of any disease. These are some special qualities of Ram Rajya. It is said that in the reign of Lord Sri Ram no one was suffering from the natural, physical and spiritual pain. They all were doing their duties well, lovingly. There was no sin and no sinner. Everybody was religious minded. People were leading their life on religious ground. There were no untimely death. Everyone was of a handsome personality. Nobody was poor, pitiable and sad. There was no illiteracy. All the men and women were wise enough. They were on the right path of religion. There was no cunningness at all. Nobody was cheat at that time. There was wisdom. All of them were wise. Here kagbhushandji says that in the kingdom of Lord Sri Ram all the worldly creatures were passing their lives on a religious and pleasant way.

Goswami Tulsidas remarks that between the seven oceans and seven Islands, Lord Sri Ram was the only king there.

> भूमि सप्त सागर मेखला, एक भूप रघुपति कोसला।
> भुवन अनेक रोम प्रति जासू, यह प्रभुता कछु बहुत न तासँ।
>
> Bhoomi sapt sagar mekhla, ek bhoop Raghupati kosla.
> Bhuwan anek rom prati jasu, yeh prabhuta kuchh bahut na tasan.

The pleasure and the wealth of Ram Rajya was in such a quantity that even Sharda who is the goddess of wisdom and Sesh Nag can not be able to describe.

> राम राजकर सुख संपदा।
> वरनि न सकइ फनीस सारदा॥
>
> Ram rajkar sukh sampada.
> Varni na sakai fanis sarda.

In Ram Rajya, everybody was kind hearted. There was no selfishness anywhere. All the trees were giving fruits in every season. The lions and elephants were living at the same place. All the wild animals were living side by side with love. There was no enmity in them. the pleasant wind blew in every season. The cows were giving milk according to the demand of the people. In Tretayug there was the atmosphere of Satyug. The mountains were producing all type of jewels. The rivers were watery in every season. The ocean were leaving precious stones on their shores during tides and people were becoming rich and rich on getting those precious stones. The sun was giving heat according to the need of the people. In Ram Rajya the clouds were giving water on the demand of the people according to their need. Lord Sri Ram has done many Aswamedh Yagya in his time. He denoted several things to the Brahmans. His beloved wife Sita was always ready to follow her husband. She knew it well that Lord Sri Ram is super human, so she served him as she could.

> पति अनुकूल सदा सीता, सोभा खानि सुसील विनीता।
> जानत कृपा सिंधु प्रभुताई, सेवत चरन कमल मन लाई॥
> जद्यपि गृह सेवक सेवकिनी, विपुल सदा सेवा विधि गुनी।
> निजकर गृह परिचरजा करई, रामचन्द्र आयसु अनुसरई॥

Pati anukool sada Sita, sobha khani susil vineeta.
Janat kripa sindhu prabhutai, sevat charan kamal man layi
Jadhyapi grih sevak sevkini, vipul sada seva vidhi guni.
Nijkar grih paricharja karai, Ramchandra aayasu anusari

Though there were several servants in the palace but Sita always did her work with her own hands. She used to serve all her mothers without being proud. Actually Sitaji was not an ordinary woman. Uma, Rama, and Brahmani etc. were always worshipping and willing to get the mercy of Goddess Sita. Mother Sita is serving the feet of Lord Sri Ram in a usual way without any hesitation. All the brothers were always busy in the service of Sri Ram. There was great love for their brothers in the heart of Sri Ram. Sri Ram always used to preach his brothers for good deeds. People were leading a happy and prosperous life. In the meantime, a great happening took place. It is said that once Lord Sri Ram were wandering in the streets of Ayodhya in disguise to take the welfare of his subjects. He saw that a washerman was beating his wife for her mistakes. He was taunting on Sri Ram saying that I am not Ram, who had accepted the wife, who had been out for a long time from him. In the meantime he heard these words of that very washerman. He heard well all his taunts and thought within himself about his deeds. Ram thought out a plan. He determined to leave Sita forever. So he asked Laxman to take Sita with him and to leave her in the ashram of the Rishi Balmiki in the forest. Laxman did the same. Laxman prepared a chariot. He got seated Sita in it. He took her in the ashram of Balmiki and left her there in the pregnant condition. Even Sita was also unknown about all these. She could not understand the reason to this behaviour of Sri Ram. She could not understand her fault. She wept and wept bitterly, but Laxman left her in the forest and came back to Ayodhya. He himself was not knowing the secret of this. But he followed the order of Sri Ram. When Rishi Balmiki came to know that Sita, the daughter of king Janak, the daughter-in-law of king Dashratha and beloved wife of Lord Sri Ram has come in his ashram, he took her in his ashram. He asked his wife to take care Sita as their daughter. He knew it well that Sita is not an ordinary woman. She is the mother of whole universe. He also knew about her extra ordinary qualities.

जनक सुता जगजननि जानकी, अतिसय प्रिय करूना निधान की।
ताके युग पद कमल मनावउँ, जासु कृपा निर्मल मति पावउँ॥

Janak suta jagjanni Janki, atisay priya karuna nidhan ki.
Take yug pad kamal manavayun, jasu kripa nirmal mati pavayun.

Time passed. Gradually Sita forgot her sadness with the time. She could only remember her own Ram by heart but could do nothing to get him. She was undone.

On the other hand, when Sri Ram had sent Sita to the forest, he never laughed. He could not express his ideas before anyone, because nobody knew this fact. Even Lord Sri Ram could not express his idea before his brothers and mothers also. All the mothers and brothers were wonder-struck to see his behaviour and this situation of Sri Ram. His daily routine was disturbed. Yet he always tried to pose his happiness. Nobody could feel the grief of his heart.

There in the forest Mother Sita gave birth to two sons. They were named Lava and Kush by Rishi Balmiki. Both were so handsome like their father and so brave as Sri Ram himself. Gradually they grew young. Rishi Balmiki gave them all type of education in the ashram. They were well educated. By the mercy of Guru Balmiki they both become famous archer. Once Sri Ram did an Ashwamedh Yagya. Ashwamedh Yagya is such a ceremony in which a horse is left to go anywhere. he soldiers of the same king followed the horse. If anyone tries to catch the horse, they fight against them. Thus wherever the horse goes that area comes under control of that king who had done the Ashwamedh yagya. In this way that area comes in the kingdom of that very king. In that very yagya he left a horse. The horse ran for a long distance. When it reached near the ashram of Rishi Balmiki, Lava and Kush saw a beautiful charming horse was grazing near the ashram. They caught it. There was a huge army behind the horse to protect it. So the soldiers opposed this. They asked the children to leave the horse. but they did not leave it. The soldiers requested the children no to do so, but they did not heed them. Now unwillingly the soldiers challenged them to fight. Only two children defeated the whole army. Everyone was wonder-struck to see the most powerful children before them. They had never seen such a bravery. At this Bharat and Shatrughan came for battle. A fierce battle took place. And even Bharat and Shatrughan were also defeated. When Laxman came to know about the wonderful task of the children, he became very angry Laxman came before the children and asked them to leave the horse. The boys did not agree to leave the horse without battle. Thus, Laxman challenged them to be ready for battle. A fierce battle took place between Laxman and Lava-Kush. They fought bravely. Laxman was injured and fainted in the battlefield. Now there was a great hue and cry. The news went to Ayodhya, that only two children have caught the horse of Ashwamegdh Yagya and they have defeated the whole army. They have also defeated even Laxman, Bharat and Shatrughan in the battle. When Sri Ram heard this news, he became very anxious to see those the bravest of brave.

Sri Ram rode on his chariot and went there in the forest. From a distance he saw those two young children, who had defeated the whole army. They were standing near the horse. He was wonder-struck to see such a handsome boys in the forest. He could not understand the fact. Sri Ram asked the children that why they have caught the horse? They answered gently that the horse is so attractive and beautiful. It was grazing near our Ashram, so we have caught it. The soldiers, who were guarding it, they challenged us, so we have answered them in retreat. Hearing the sweet words of the children Sri Ram laughed at them. But when he saw that his dear brothers Bharat, Shatrughan and Laxman are lying senseless on the ground, he could not check his anger. He took the bow and arrow in his hands and challenged the children for battle. As they got ready to fight, Rishi Balmiki heard this noise and came there. He saw that Lord Sri Ram himself is ready for battle against his sons. He stood firm like a rock between them and told Sri Ram about the children. He introduced those children and said Lava and Kush the two children are your own sons. So my Lord Ram, it is not proper for you that you fight against your own sons. When Sri Ram came to know the fact, he came forward. He threw his bow and arrow aside and embraced Lava and Kush. In the meantime, Laxman, Bharat and Shatrughan also stood up. As they found that those children are the sons of Lord Sri Ram. They were much pleased at their bravery. Mother Sita also came there. In this way Sri Ram took them with their mother to Ayodhya. Sri Ram ruled over Ayodhya for a long period. According to Goswami Tulsidas, Sri Ram ruled over the seventh Islands.

सप्तद्वीप सागर मेखला, एक भूप रघुपति कोसला।
Saptadwipa sagar mekhala, ek bhoop Raghupati kausala.

All the brothers had two sons, who were handsome and brave like their parents. The fact is this, that the almighty Lord is behaving like a human being though he is beyond the reach of our thinking. With all their brothers, Sri Ram used to take bath daily in the pious water of river Saryu. They sat in the court and listen to the lines of Vedas and Purans.

Everybody was praising the fate of Awadhpuri, where Sri Ram used to live. Rishi Narad, Sanak Sanadan Sanatkumar used to come to ayodhya daily to see and worship their Lord Ram. When they visited the city, they forgot all the worldly things. The white coloured high structural buildings of Ayodhya were touching the sky. The diamonds were arranged in the palace to give light in the night inspite of lamps. The kitchen gardens were filled with different types of flowers. Sweet and low wind blew in every season. There was autumn like season throughout the whole year. The markets of Ayodhya were well decorated. Even Kuber, the master of wealth was also ashamed to see the richness of Ayodhya. The place where king Ram, the husband of goddess Laxmi rules, no one can describe the richness of that place. All type of pleasure and wealth was spread in Ayodhya.

People were remembering the virtues of Lord Sri Ram from place to place. Here goswami Tulsidas describes the kindness of Sri Ram, who had taken birth for the protection of saints and for the destruction of bad elements from the earth. In this way, all the men and women of Ayodhya are worshipping Lord Sri Ram and he used to think good and do good for the welfare of their subjects.

Once Sri Ram with all their brothers came to see the beautiful garden. There came Sankadik rishies, who were in the age of child. They worshipped many times to Lord Sri Ram. They begged for devotion to Sri Ram. When Sankadik rishies went away, Hanuman touched the feet of Sri Ram and said that Bharat wants to request you for something. Sri Ram replied, there is nothing as secret for Bharat. Bharat could ask for anything. Hearing such words of Lord Sri Ram, Bharat bowed low in his feet and spoke gently. He requested to tell him the difference between saint and evil doers. Sri Ram said, listen Bharat! there are many symptoms of saints which are described in the Vedas and Purans. Take a little example of it. The character and behaviour of saints and evil doers are like an axe and sandal plant. The axe cuts the plant of the sandal with cruelty. But even then the sandal plants give its essence to the axe. This is the reason that the piece of sandal is used in the worship of God and the steal is burnt in the fire and on becoming red it is beaten by the iron smith, as a punishment of its bad deeds. The saints are kind hearted. They are merciful on poors. They are worshipper of God by body, mind and soul, without any greed. The saints have no proud of any thing.

संत हृदय नवनीत समाना, कहा कविन्ह पर कहै न जाना।
नित दुख द्रवत सदा नवनीता, पर दुख द्रवइ सो संत पुनीता॥
Sant hriday navneet samaana, kaha kavinh par kahayi na jaana.
Nit dukh dravat sada navneeta, par dukh dravai so sant puneeta.

He says, well Bharat! Such type of creatures are most lovable for me. They are my life. The saints have a great devotion in my feet, they never think about sex and other worldly pleasure. Simplicity, reality, and friendship is deeply rooted in their blood. The saints always remain pleased. They follow the principle of religion. The saints have a great love in the feet of the Brahmans. They pay regard to Ganga and Gayatri. They never go back from their principles. The saints never use harsh words. They speak sweet words. The saints never mind for their fame or defame. They do not care for their profit and loss. They have great love towards me. The persons of such nature are good hearted for me. I like them as my life itself. They lead a pleasant life. Everyone gives regard to saints and sages.

Now please listen to the distinction of evil doers. Mind about the nature of the wrong persons.

परहित घृत तिन्ह के मन माखी।
जे पर दोष लखहिं सरसाखी॥
Parhit ghrit tinha ke man makhi,
Je par dosh lakhahin sarsakhi.

One should never accompany them. The company of the wrong persons is always painful. They always prejudice to see the others wealth. By nature these people are sexy, angry, greedy and proud. They always wear the skin of cruelty and cleverness. Unnecessarily they make enmity with others, either he is a well wisher of them or not. These people always tell a lie. Such type of people are sweet speaking but of cunning nature. Such evil hearted persons are always selfish. Their behaviour is always against the family. They are of raudy nature. They do not recognise their parents, teachers and Brahmans. These people never live in the company of saints and sages. They always behave against the religion. These people always oppose everybody. They are the centre of proud and cunningness. In Satyug, there were very few persons of evil thoughts. In Tretayug, the evil doers were found somewhere and in Dwaperyug the number of evil doers increased step by step. There were a large number of demons like Ravan, Ahiravan and so on. But in Kaliyug, maximum people are behaving like demons. Their way of life, their way of eating and treating is also animal like. In this age, the behaviour of people is unnatural.

Once Sri Ram called his Guru, Brahman and other citizens to him. They all sat near him. Now Sri Ram said, "Only that person is my devotee and lovable, who follows my discipline without any hesitation. If I say some thing against the society, you people can forbade me without any fear."

जौ अनीजि कछु भाखौं भाई, तौ मोहि बरजेहु भय बिसराई।
Jo aniji kachu baakho bhai, tau mohi barajehu bhaya bisrayi.

He further told, that we have gotten this human life by great penance. This human physique is not available even to the gods also. All of our religious books tell us the dignity of human life. This human body is the boat to cross Bhawasagar. All the impossible things are made possible by this human body. On behalf of my mercy, one can go across the Bhawasagar by this very boat. he further told that only one thing is sufficient for the success of life. That is to serve the Brahmans by body, mind and soul. All the gods help and favour those persons who serve the feet of the Brahmans whole heatedly. I shall tell you an other secret also. Nobody could get my devotion without getting the devotion of Lord Shiva. When they all heard these sweet words of Lord Sri Ram they touched their feet and went home pleasantly.

Once Lord Shiva said to Parwati that Kagbhushandji told Garud the whole life history of Lord Sri Ram. Parwati became anxious to know the reason of this. She asked to Lord Shiva that being in the physical form of a crow, how Kagbhushandji became the devotee of Lord Sri Ram. Please tell me clearly. I am in suspense. Lord Shiva told that in thousands of people one or two can become religious minded. In crores of these religious persons only some are against the sex. Our religious books the Srutis, Vedas and Purans say that among the crores only some have systematic knowledge. The most precious thing is the devotion of Lord Sri Ram without any proud. Thus, Parwatiji asked to Lord Shiva that how the Kagbhushandji got such a type of devotion. Please tell me in detail. You please further tell me that how and where Kagbhushandji got the pious character of Lord Sri Ram. How you yourself have heard the story of Lord Sri Ram. Garud was the most wise man, who had been always in the service of God, why he went to Kagbhushandji to hear the pious history of Lord Sri Ram leaving the rishies and munies aside. Hearing the pleasant voice of Goura Parwati, Lord Shiva felt a great pleasure within the heart and said, Parwati! you are very thankful that you have so much devotion in the feet of Sri Ram. Now I shall tell you the pious life history of Lord Sri Ram. The same question was asked by Garud, the king of the birds to Kagbhushandji. You please listen attentively. I shall tell you with due respect the whole life story of Lord Sri Ram. Listen Parwati! in your previous life your name was Sati and your father's name was Daksha. Once upon a time Daksha made great yagna. Due to some reasons he had prejudice towards me so he insulted me there in his yagna where a lot of kings were gathered. There you couldn't tolerate my insult done by him and you lost your life through yoga. In this way my followers ruined that very yagna and punished them well, whoever had insulted me there. I became very sad at being apart from you. In your absence, I began to wander in the forests and hills for peace. In the meantime, I went on a hill the natural scene of that hill was very charming and attractive. That very bird, named Kagbhushandji used to live there under a Banyan tree. That place was untouched from all kind of illusions and dillusions. The crow whose name was Kagbhushandi used to tell the pious history of Sri Ram under that tree. When I saw this scene, I became anxious to stay there for some time to get mental peace.

Now please listen the reason, why did Garud go to Kagbhushandi. When Lord Sri Ram fought with Indrajeet in the battlefield, by the way Indrajeet fastened and tied him in Nagpash. He was not able to move even a single inch from their place. When Rishi Narad saw it, he, at once requested Garud to go and cut the tie of Sri Ram. Now as Garud came there in the battlefield, he, at once, ate all the snakes and thus he set free Lord Sri Ram. Garud came back. But on the way he began to think that the almighty God who is the creator of all the worldly things, how he could be tightened in Nagpash. He is beyond the reach of anyone. Garud was perplexed at this he could not understand the fact. He was proud of himself. So he went to Rishi Narad and told about his worries. Rishi Narad laughed and said, you are disturbed like me. Once upon a time, I also suffered from this purplexion. This is the illusion of Sri Ram. Nobody could understand this at all. You please go to Bramah. Only Bramah can guide you for this. He went to Bramahlok. Bramah sent him to Lord Shiva. Thus, he came to me and told all what had happened. Then I told him that it needs your brain wash. It is possible only when you get concern of saints and sages and listen to the discussion about the virtues of Lord Sri Ram. In this way, I sent him to Kagbhushandji to listen the story of Lord Sri Ram. He went there and saw that different type of birds are coming and listening the life history of Sri Ram. As Garud was about to start his preaching, at the same time king of the birds Garud reached there. The whole of the birds stood up in honour of Garud. Even Kagbhushandi also arose and welcomes him, he asked the welfare of Garud and seated him on a high place. Now the crow spoke gently, we all are thankful today by seeing you in our company. Please tell me the reason of your reaching here. How may I help you? Garud said, I am very thankful to see you. Please listen to my request. On seeing your Ashram all my delusions have gone away. My brain is washed. Now my mind is fresh. So please tell me something, about the pious life history of Lord Sri Ram. Hearing the sweet and pleasant voice of Garud Kagbhushandji became very please and started telling the pious history of Ram Charit.

Kaghushandi told him that how Rishi Narad became anxious to get married. He further told about the birth of Ravan. He also told Garud that why God himself has incarnated on the earth of Ayodhya, in the palace of king Dashratha. He further told in detail about the childhood of Sri Ram. Step by step he told about the arrival of Rishi Vishwamitra in the palace of king Dashratha. He thoroughly told all about the marriage of Lord Sri Ram with Sita. He told about the scene of coronation of Lord Sri Ram. Again he told in brief how the pleasure of Ayodhya was turned into grief. He also told word by word about the sadness of the countrymen and the discussion between Sri Ram and Laxman. How and when Sri Ram went to the forest, how he crossed the pious river Ganga with the help of Kewat and stayed at Prayag. He described about the meeting of Rishi Balmiki with Lord Sri Ram and why he stayed at Chittrakoot. The crow told Garud that how Sumantra goes to inform Bharat and Shatrughan about the death of king Dashratha and how Bharat tried to take him back to Ayodhya. He also told that how Lord Sri Ram pacified Bharat and how Bharat came back from Chittrakoot to Ayodhya taking the sandal of Lord Sri Ram. Bharat left all their princely dress and began to live like a saint in Nandi village. He also told Garud that how Rishi Attri met to Lord Sri Ram in the forest. He said how Sri Ram killed the most powerful demon Biradh and how Muni Sarbhang left his body by yoga.

He has shown everyone the love of Suteeckchhan in the feet of Lord Sri Ram and told about the discussion with Rishi August.

Kagbhushandji told Garud that why and how demon king Ravan had stolen Sita from the ashram. He told that when Ravan was taking away Sita by Viman then hearing the pity words of Sita how the vulture king Jatayu tried to save Sita and dedicated him for the service of Lord Ram.

He further told that how Jatayu was badly injured with the sword of Ravan and how Sri Ram made his funeral by his own hands. Sri Ram killed the demon Kabandha and ate fruits in the ashram of Sabari. He told about the discussion of Sri Ram and Rishi Narad. He told that how Hanuman met with Sri Ram. With the help of Hanuman they made friendship with Sugreeva and killed his elder brother Bali who was a great sinner. After coronation of Sugreeva, Sri Ram stayed at mountain Pravarsan for some months. He also described the importance of rainy season in our life. Kagbhushandji told Garud that how Sugreeva sent the monkeys and bears to search out Sita. In the forest Sampati the elder brother of Jatayu met them and he told them all about Sita. He told how Hanuman crossed the ocean. In the form of a mosquito he entered in Lanka and pacified mother Sita. Hanuman ruined the gardens of Ravan, taught a lesson to Ravan, burnt his kingdom Lanka which was made of gold and came back to Sri Ram. All of the monkeys came to Sri Ram and told him the welfare of mother Sita.

Kagbhushandi also told garud that how Raghunath crossed the ocean with all of their army. Now Angad went to Ravan as an ambassador to convince him not to be rigid for war. He told how the monkeys fought against the demons and they got victory over Kumbhakaran and Meghnad. It is said that lacks of sons and crores of the family members of Ravan were killed in that war.

एक लाख पूत सवा लाख नाती।
तेहि रावन घर दिया न बाती॥
Ek lakh poot, sawa lakh nati.
Tehi Rawan ghar, diya na bati.

The great war between Ram and Ravan was described by Kagbhushandji word by word. He further told that the tyrant demon king Ravan was killed by Sri Ram and his younger brother Vibishan became the king of Lanka. In this way all of the gods became fearless and please. He told about the meeting of Sita and Raghupati, where the gods worshipped and prayed them.

Lord Sri Ram came back to Ayodhya at the appointed time riding on Pushpak viman with all of his army commanders. At last Kagbhushandi described in detail all about the coronation of Lord Sri Ram. He also told about the goodness of Ram Rajya. Lord Shiva says to Parwatiji that the story which I have told you, Kagbhushandi told it all to Garud. When Garud heard the life history of Lord Sri Ram he spoke pleasantly, that by hearing the story of Lord Sri Ram all my delusion has gone away. Now the devotion in the feet of Sri Ram has increased in my mind. Garud said that there was a misunderstanding in my heart to see Sri Ram tightened by Nagpash in the battlefield. I was much worried that why Lord Sri Ram is feeling purplexion. In the battlefield the behaviour or Lord Sri Ram was like a common man. So when I saw him in such a miserable position, I felt suspense. Now that very suspension has gone away. I think, if the delusion would have not come in my mind, it was impossible for me to see such a great devotee of Lord Sri Ram.

Kagbhushandi said to Garun that you are praiseworthy for me because you are the nearest and dearest of Lord Sri Ram. There was no delusion or love in your mind. Only you have come here to show your mercy on me. In the words of Goswami Tulsidas, Kagbhushandi says to Garud that you have told me about your own frustration, but there is no matter to wonder about it. Goswami Tulsidas is called **Trikal Darshi**. He had a great knowledge of past, present and future. So in challenging words Tulsidasji says that Rishi Narad, Brahma, Sanad-Sanandan and Santkumar other great saints and sages have also become blind by the influence of love and sex, that is maya. Everyone likes to collect for future. Nobody can escape themselves from the influence of greed. The richness has ruined the fair mind of the gentlemen and the greatness has made deaf everyone. And there is no one in the world who could escape themselves from the cut motion of the young lady.

को अस जगत विमल वैरागा, नारि नयन सर जाहि न लागा।
Ko as jagat vimal vaiyraga, naari nayan sar Jahi na laga.

These are a number of family illusions the "Maya" whose power is beyond the description. Even Brahma and Shiva were also afraid from this Maya. So other lives have no value at all. That maya is the slave of Raghunathji. No one could escape themselves from Maya without the mercy of Lord Sri Ram. Nobody could perceive the character of Maya, which has influenced the whole world. All the worldly creatures are dancing under the influence of Maya. The God, who is almighty, omnipresent and omnipotent. Who is above all. Who is the creator of the universe. The supreme power has incarnated the physical feature of a king. He has done all this activities like a human being. That almighty plays different role at the stage but actually he is not that in real sense.

Kagbhushandji says to Garud that these virtues of Lord Sri Ram are demoralising the demons and make pleasant to the devotees. The persons who are of dull mind and who are very sexual they blame even God also. The person whose eye sight is disturbed, the moon looks to him of yellow colour. The person who had forgotten the direction, in fact he used to say that the sun rises in the west. Actually such type of people feel suspecious by nature, they think that their mind is very superior, the Lord, the God himself is wrong, his activities are wrong. In this way the person who are under the influence of sex, anger, proud and greed, they are suffering from the home sickness and they are lying in the deep dark well. So how they may be able to know the character of Lord Sri Ram. Kagbhushandji said to Garud that, according to my reach, I have told you the story of Lord Sri Ram. He told, once upon a a time I also felt suspense about the greatness of Lord Sri Ram, I will tell you the whole story in brief because you are the most devotee of Lord Sri Ram.

He further said, listen please Garun! Whenever Lord Sri Ram incarnates himself in the Human form and acts in many ways for the welfare of our devotees, then often I come to Ayodhya to see the child like behaviour of Lord Sri Ram. That handsome child Ram is the centre of my devotion. Honourable Garud, then I feel happy to see the charming face of our Lord Sri Ram. In disguise, I became the crow and saw the child activities of Sri Ram in the childhood, wherever they go in the palace of Dashratha, I flew with him. And wherever they drop the loaf of bread on the ground I used to eat it pleasantly. Once when he was a mere child, he sat on the floor which was shining like the diamond. He saw their own reflection and began to dance. He began to play with me in many ways. On laughing when they run towards me to catch me, I flew away. Then he began to laugh but when I went far, they started weeping. When I go near him to touch the feet, he began to look here and there. Seeing the child like behaviour of Lord Sri Ram a suspense came in my mind that being almighty what type of behaviour our Lord is doing?

I thought in this way, you please Garud realise on me, Sri

Ram motivated maya and it influenced me by all sides. That maya could not pain me like the other creatures. When Sri Ram recognised my worriness, he laughed. But no one could see him in this position. Even the four brothers and their parents could not understand this secret. He again ran to catch me with their lotus like fingers. Then I tried to fly away but Sri Ram raised his arms to catch me. I flew so long in the sky. But as I saw back, I found that his hands are near me. I flew high in the sky and again when I looked back, I found that the little hands of Sri Ram are following me there also. I flew so far as I could but when I turned back to see, I found those hands nearby me. I became senseless to see this fact.

As I closed my eyes with a great fear, I found myself in Ayodhya again. Sri Ram smiled to see me. As well as he smiled with a laugh, I entered in his mouth. Well Garud! You please have faith in me, in their stomach I saw several universes. There were many worlds which were different in shape and construction. I saw there crores of Brahmas and crores of Shiva. Countless stars, sun and moons were found there. There were thousands of mountains, earth, several oceans, rivers and tanks. I saw there such types of things which I have never seen in the whole world. I am unable to describe about those wonderful things. In this way in every universe I stayed therefore one hundred years. Thus, I wandered there for a long time. There were different types of Ayodhya and the residents were also different in physique. The river Saryu which flows near by Ayodhya, was also seen in its different form. There I saw king Dashratha and mother Kaushilya and all the brothers in several forms. I found that Sri Ram has incarnated himself in every universe and I saw his child like behaviour in the same way. With the effect of illusion, I saw the same childhood of Lord Sri Ram in every universe. It appeared that several years have passed in wandering in the every universe. In the stomach of Lord Sri Ram I saw many worlds which is worth praising. I thought within myself that my mind is perturbed and disturbed. Within few hours I saw all these. There appeared suspension in my mind. In this way, when Lord Sri Ram saw me in worries, he laughed. At the same time I came out from his mouth. Thus, he began to play with me in the same child like manner. I tried my best to console my heart but I could not succeed. I put my mouth on the ground and become unconscious. I remembered Lord Sri Ram by heart when he saw me in such a pitiable condition, he checked his Maya. He touched my head by his hands and in this way he turned all my grief into pleasure. Tears appeared in my eyes. I prayed to Sri Ram. He felt pity on me. Sri Ram spoke in a grand sound that Kagbhushandi you can ask me for any type of blessing what you want. You can get all the worldly pleasure. Now I requested Sri Ram to give me his devotion. Sri Ram said, O.K. He praised me for my cleverness. There is no comparison of your fate in the whole world, because you have asked me the devotion which is the centre of all pleasure. Lord Sri Ram further said that listen please Kagbhushandi now all type of good virtues will reside in your heart by my mercy. You will come to know automatically about devotion, knowledge, science, yoga and vairagya and its secrets. By my blessing no disturbance and no maya could influence your mind. Now the illusion may not influence you.

In this way, in the pleasant mood, Sri Ram said to Kagbhushandi that I shall tell you my own principle. Listen to me carefully to what I say leave all the worldly things aside and remember me by heart. The whole of the world has been created by my Maya, in which different type of creatures live. All are lovable for me because I have made them all. But I like human being most. Among them I like Brahman, yet the learned Brahman is most loving for me who follows the principles of Dharam. The person who passes his life in the service of Mankind, he stands in the first rank of my lovers. Even of the below status person is also my devotee, he is as lovable for me as my life itself. Thus, Sri Ram suggested me to pray and remember him leaving all type of hopes and faith aside. He further told that if you will remember me every moment by heart. Sudden death may not come to you. Hearing the sweet and pious words of Lord Sri Ram I became pleased. He pacified me in many ways and again he began to play like a child. In the mean time mother Kaushilya came there. She took him in her arms. Kagbhushandji praises the fate of the citizens of Ayodhya and says that the pleasure to live with Sri Ram, is beyond the reach of Rishies and Munies, every citizen of Ayodhya enjoys it in a common way. He said, after passing some time in Ayodhya I came back to my ashram. Since then the illusion could not influence me from when Raghunath has accepted me. He said, well Garud this is my personal experience that, without the mercy of Lord Sri Ram and without his devotion no body can escape himself from worldly pains. He said that there is nothing as additional by my side, but I have seen all these with my own eyes.

In this way hearing the pleasant words of Kagbhushandji,

Garud felt great pleasure and raised his feathers up. Now the influence of Lord Sri Ram came in his heart. He had treated Sri Ram as a common man, so when He came to know this fact that he is almighty and endless God he was much ashamed within himself. Thus, Goswami Tulsidas finally says that nobody can cross the Bhawasagar without Guru.

गुरू बिन भव निधि तरै न कोई, जौ विरंचि संकर सम होई।
Guru bin bhav nidhi tarai na koi, jou virinchi sankar sam hoi.

Garud politely requested to Kagbhushandji to clear a little confusion also which has raised in his mind. He asked that you are the most lovable devotee of Sri Ram then what is the reason that you are in crow body (physique)? Lord Shiva has also told me that you will be alive upto last time of this creation (universe). But as far as I know all the worldly creatures will have to ruin either today or after some time. So please tell me in detail also that how and here you have come to know about the secret life story of Lord Sri Ram. Hearing the words of Garud, Kagbhushandji became very pleased and thanked Garud for such type of question. He said that I have gotten the devotion of Lord Sri Ram in this very physique. So I love this body too much.

एहि तन राम भगति मैं पाई।
ताते मोहि ममता अधिकाई॥
Aehi tan Ram bhagati mein payi,
Tate mohi mamta adhikaye.

I am not in favour to loose this body because without body no devotion could be done. And without devotion life is worthless. He further told that I have roamed in several lives but I could get no satisfaction. I am much pleased and satisfied now a days in this form.

Now I shall tell you some thing about my pre-birth. Firstly, when I took birth, that was the age of Kaliyug. I was born in a below status family. I was the devotee of only Lord Shiva. I used to abuse the other gods due to proudness. Though I was born in Ayodhya but I was totally unknown about its significance. I was very talkative by nature. I was also proud of my knowledge and wisdom. Now I have come to know the significance of Ayodhya which has been described in Vedas and Purans. Only then the person can come to know the significance of ayodhya, when Lord Sri Ram will reside in his heart with the bow and arrow in their hands. Thus, that very Kaliyug was so painful for every one because every body was involved in sin and wrong deeds. In Kaliyug, all the religions and religious books will go lost. People had searched out several ways by their own imaginations. So I shall tell you now some activities of people which is being done in Kaliyug.

वरन धर्म नहिं आश्रम चारी, श्रुति विरोध रत सब नर नारी।
द्विज श्रुति बेचक भूप प्रजासन, नहिं कोउ मान निगम अनुसासन॥

Varan dharam nahin ashram chari, shruti virodh rat sab nar nari.
Davij shruti beehak bhupi prajasan, nahi kou man nigam anushasan.

The four varnas and four ashramas will go ruin in this age. People will act against the rules of our Vedas and Puranas. Brahmans will try to sell the main religious books. In Kaliyug, everyone will go their own way. The persons who believed in pomp and show, only he will be called true saint. Those persons who tell a lie in every walk of life, people will call them virtuous man. Eat, drink and be merry will be the principle of life of the common people. The person who is of a boasting nature, he would be the great orator and leader in Kaliyug.

Mostly people will be henpacked. They will dance under the controls of their wives in the same way, as the monkeys dance according to the wish of their master.

नारी विवस नर सकल गोसाई, नाचहिं नर मर्कट की नाई।

Nari vivas nar sakal gosain, nachahin nar markat ki nai.

People will oppose gods, the Brahmans, the Vedas and the saints. The women will try to satisfy their sex with other people, leaving their handsome husband aside.

सब नर काम लोभ रत क्रोधी, देव विप्र श्रुति संत विरोधी।
गुन मंदिर सुन्दरपति त्यागी, भजहिं नारी पर पुरूष अभागी।

Sab nar kam lobh rat krodhi, dev vipra shruti sant virodhi
Gun mandir sundarpati tyagi, bhajahin nari par purush abhagi.

Inspite of teaching about our Indian culture and civilisation the parents will teach and preach their children to work for the stomach.

मातु पितु बालकन्ह बोलावहिं, उदर भरै सोइ धर्म सिखावहिं।

Matu pitu balkanh bolavahin, udar bahrai soi dharain sikhavahin

Kagbhushandi says that I have seen the character of Kaliyug because the persons who are going on wrong paths, they will be called wise. Such people create the hindrance in the way of those persons, who follow the religious path. In Kaliyug, the saints and sages will go rich and the householders will became poor and poor. It will be the character of Kaliyug that the sons will follow their parents only upto then, until they do not see the face of their wives.

सुत मानहि मात पिता तब लौं, अबलानन दीख नहीं जब लौं।
ससुरारि पियारी लगी जब तें, रिपु रूप कुटुम्ब भये तब तें॥
नहि मान पुरान न वेदहि जो, हरि सेवक संत सही कलि सो।
कलि बारहि बार दुकाल परै, बिनु अन्नदुखी सब लोग मरै॥

Sut manahi mat pita tab laun, ablanan deekh nahin tab laun.
Sasurari piyari lagi jab ten, ripu roop kutumb bhaye tab ten.
Nahi man puran na vedahi jo, hari sevak sant sahi kaliso.
Kali barahi bar dukal parai, binu anndukhi sab log marai.

In this age the kings will be sinner, they will not follow the religious paths, they will always try to punish, to crush or to suck their subjects. Only he will be the true saint in Kaliyug, who will always oppose the Vedas and Purans. In Kaliyug, a large number of people will die of hunger due to natural havoc. Kaghbushandi says to Garud that the whole universe will full be of cunningness, jealousy, boasting, proud, sex, pomp and show etc. There will be part rain and due to this the seeds will not grow in a proper way.

In this age, people will start fighting each other without any purpose. People would think in such a way that they have to live long on this earth, but on actual speaking, their life is very short. The beggary will spread out as a business by the people of every caste. People will become selfish. They would criticise every one and every religion.

Well Garud, please listen, inspite of several short comings, there are some goodness of this Kaliyug also. With a little effort people can get their aim of life. They may achieve their goal the Moksha by a little effort. In other ages like Satyug, Tretayug, Dwaparyug, people achieve Moksha by hard penance. But in Kaliyug they will get Moksha only by remembering the pious name of Sri Ram.

कलियुग सम युग आन नहि, जौ नर कर विस्वास।
गाइ राम गुन गन विमल, भव तर विनहि प्रयास॥

Kaliyug sam yug aah nahi, jau nar kar viswas.
Gayi Ram gun gan vimal, bhav tar virati prayas.

Thus, if we have faith by all respect then there is no any better yug as Kaliyug. Because by singing the virtues of Lord Sri Ram people can go across the Bhawasagar without any effort. Goswami Tulsidasji says that there are four main steps of religion, but in Kaliyug only one religion is important, that is donation. In this age, if people donate anything any how, it proves as a blessing for them. In this way the people who become the devotee of Lord Sri Ram by body, mind and soul, they never come under the influence of any Yug Dharm. Kagbhushandi says to Garud that in that very Kalikal I stayed in Ayodhya for a long time. Due to natural havoc and poverty I went so far from there for livelihood. Listen Garud I went to Ujjain. At that time I was in a very miserable condition. Time passed and I earned some money there. There also I was the devotee of Lord Shiva. There was a Brahman in Ujjain. His nature was very simple. He was very kind. He had adopted the Vedic pattern of life. He was also devotee of Lord Shiva. I made him my Guru there. Seeing my gentle behaviour the Brahman began to teach me like their own son. He gave me Sambhu Mantra and preached me in many ways. I began to remember that very Sambhu Mantra in the temple of Lord Shiva. I was much proud of my devotion. I had taken birth in a below status family. I was a man of mean mentality so I was jealous with other devotees, Brahman and even with the other gods also. Seeing my bad conduct the Guru used to preach me daily not to do like this.

Kagbhushandji told to Garud that once upon a time I was remembering the Sambhu Mantra in a temple of Lord Shiva. By chance my Guru came there in that temple. Due to proud I could not pay proper respect to him and I did not salute him. The Guru was so simple that he did not mind about my behaviour. But Lord Shiva could not bear the dishonour of the Guru, because it was against the religious setup. An unseen voice came from the temple. Lord Shiva said, the persons who will oppose and insult their guru, they will go to hell many times. He said for me that you are sitting like a boa and you have not saluted your Guru, so you the sinner, you will became snake. The Guru was wonder-struck to hear this unseen voice. The

Guru bowed low on the feet of Lord Shiva and began to pray him in a polite manner. He prayed Lord Shivaji for a long time. Hearing his prayer Lord Shiva became please at the Guru. He blessed him. The Brahman requested Lord Shiva to be polite on me and asked for my welfare. Lord Shiva told and forbade me not to insult the Brahman and Guru in any way in further life. Lord Shiva said:

सुनु मम वचन सत्य अब भाई, हरि तोषन व्रत द्विज सेवकाई।
अवजनि करेहु विप्र अपमाना, जानेसु संत अनंत समाना॥

Sun mama vachan satya ab aayi, hari toshan vrat dwij sewakayi.
Aavajani karehu vipra apmana, janesu sant anant samaana.

In this way, I took birth in several forms. After a long run I found human body again. When I grew young my parents taught me some religious things. With the effect of the mercy of Lord Shiva I became the devotee of Lord Sri Ram. So on behalf of the preaching of my Guru I was in support of Sagun Brahma that is Sakar Brahma. Here Sagun Brahma means to see God face to face. When we sit for the devotion of God, with our inner eyes we see the image of God. This type of devotion is called the devotion of Sagun Brahma. It is said that through this devotion one can see God, talk to God and can feel the presence of God before him. He can see God face to face. I was always against of Nirgun Brahma. Here Nirgun brahma means such type of devotion where God is worshipped without any physical form. Here is an idea or imagination of endless and omnipresent God. Thus, the devotion of Lord Sri Ram increased in my heart day by day. One day I met Rishi Lomas in the forest under a Banyan tree. I bowed low in his feet and requested him to tell me more about the devotion of Sagun Brahma. hearing my gentle words Rishi Lomas preached me more about the different type of devotion. He said that the supreme power is omnipresent. He is almighty. He is formless. He is beyond our reasoning power. He is endless. He further told me that God is only the matter of faith, not the matter of discussion. In this way Rishi Lomas preached me in many ways. He told me again and again about Nirgun Brahma. But I touched his feet and requested to preach me about the Sagun Brahma. I further requested him to tell that way of devotion by which I can see Lord Sri Ram with my naked eyes. Firstly I shall see my Lord Sri Ram then I may follow your Nirgun philosophy. Thus, when I made cross question about Sagun and Nirgun Brahma, the Rishi became angry on me. He cursed me to become a crow. I bowed my head in the feet of the Rishi and flew away. Seeing my gentleness the Rishi called me back to him. His heart filled with gratitude. He felt pity on me. He seated me by his side and gave me "Ram Mantra".

Rishi Lomas told me much more about the childhood of Lord Sri Ram. He kept me with him for some time and told me "Sri Ram Charit Manas" there in detail.

> मुनि मोहि कछुक काल वहँ राखा, राम चरितमानस तब भाषा॥
> Muni mohi kachuka kaal vahan rakha,
> Ram Charit Manas tab bhasha.

He told me the whole life history of Lord Sri Ram and said gently, I have also gotten this secret "Ram Charitra" by the blessings of Lord Shiva, when I found you a great devotee of Lord Sri Ram only then I have described all these before you. He asked me not to tell this story before that person who has no love, no faith and no devotion of Lord Sri Ram. I bowed low in the feet of Rishi Lomas. He blessed me to be a great devotee of Lord Sri Ram. He also blessed me to be immortal. He told me that wherever you will live in your Ashram, the influence of Maya could not effect you upto one yojan that is twelve kilometres.

> जेहि आश्रम तुम्ह बसब पुनि सुमिरत श्री भगवंत।
> ब्यापिहि तहँ न अविद्या, जोजन एक प्रजंत॥
> Jehi ashram tumha basab puni sumirat shri bagwant
> Byapihi tahan na aavidya, jojan ek prajant.

The Rishi blessed me for the devotion of God. He said to me that you will come to know all secret things about the life of Lord Sri Ram. Whatever you will wish, you would get very soon by the mercy of God. I touched the feet of Rishi Lomas and came back to their ashram. At this ashram, I have passed about twenty-seven Kalap. I am always singing songs about the virtues of Sri Ram and the birds come here to listen it. The devotees enjoy this prayer. Whoever comes here he gets mental peace.

Kagbhusandji said to Garud that whenever Raghunath take birth in Awadhpuri for the protection of their devotees, then I use to go to Ayodhya to see the child like behaviour of Lord Sri Ram. He said, I have told you all the story that why and how I have gotten this body of crow. This is the reason that I love this body very much. I have seen Lord Sri Ram from my own eyes. In this way my all delusions have lost. I do not want to change this body now.

ताते यह तन मोहि प्रिय, भयउ रामपद नेह।
निज प्रभु दरसन पायउँ, गये सकल संदेह॥
Tate yeh tan mohi priya, bhayau Rampad neh.
Nij prabhu darsan payau, gaye sakalsandeh.

Kagbhushandji says that the persons who work hard to get knowledge and give up devotion, they are searching goat for milk inspite of Kamdhenu. He further said to Garud that those persons who want pleasure with other means by giving up devotion are foolish and want to cross the ocean by swimming. Thus, devotion is the only factor to get Moksha.

सुनु खगेस हरि भगति बिहाई, जे सुख चाहहिं आन उपाई।
ते सठ महासिंधु बिनु तरनी, पैरि पार चाहहिं जड़ करनी॥
Sunu khages hari Bhagati bihaye, je sukh chahahin aan upayi.
Te sath mahasindhu binu tarani, pairi par chahain jad karani

Hering the heart touching words of Bushandi, Garud spoke gently. He said, by your grace there is no delusion in my heart. I have lost my confusion. I have achieved complete rest. Now I feel inner pleasure with effect of devotion.

Please be merciful on me. There is a suspense in my mind. The saints, sages and vedas say that wisdom is superior than everything in the world. Rishi Lomas had told you also its significance but you could not mind for this. You have always protested for devotion, not for wisdom. Please define the distinction of devotion and wisdom. Bhushandji became pleased to hear the words of Garud. Respectfully Bhushandji said, there is no difference between wisdom and devotion because both finish the dark side of Bhawasagar. Devotion and wisdom both give inner light to everyone.

भगति ग्यानहि नहिं कछु भेदा, उभय हरहिं भव संभव खेदा।
Bhagati gyanahi nahin kachu bheda, Ubhay Harahin bhav sambhav kheda.

But the saints says that there is very minor difference between them. Now please listen carefully, wisdom, yoga and science these are male variety. These are masculine gender. The male is powerful in all respect while female is not so powerful. She is simply rigid. Thus, you see the female is Maya the wife of God Vishnu. Vishnu Bhagwan is almighty. Here I can saw frankly on behalf of Veda and Purana. The main saints and sages are also in this favour that the women do not like to see a beautiful woman with a complete make-up. This is a matter of principle. This principle seems true in our daily life.

मोह न नारि नारि के रूपा, पन्नगरि यह रीति अनूपा।
माया भगति सनहु तुम्ह दोउ, नारि वर्ग जानह सब कोउ॥
पुनि रघुवीरहि भगति पियारी, माया खलु नर्तकी विचारी।
अस विचारी जे मुनि विग्यानी, जाचहिं भगति सकलसुख खानी॥

Moh na naari naari ke roopa, panngari yeh riti anoopa.
Maya bhagati sanahu tumh dou, naari varg janah sab kou.
Puni Raghuvirahi bhagati piyari, maya khalu nartaki vichari.
As vichari je muni vigyani, jachahin bhagati sakal sukh khani.

Thus, maya and devotion both belong to female section. The fact is this that Sri Raghunath likes to have devotion not the poor maya. Sri Ram has always preferred devotion. So maya always appears with devotion. In this way the influence of maya could not effect the devotee of Lord Sri Ram. Thus, the wise men always try to require devotion which is the centre of all the pleasure. Nobody could understand this secret of Raghunathji. And the person who has recognised the mercy of Sri Ram, he may not come under the influence of delusion in the dream also. The worldly things can not attract him. Generally the devotee passes his life in devotion.

Kagbhushandji further told that I shall tell you more about the distinction of wisdom and devotion. This story is untold. One can understand it, but cannot describe it. The creature that is life is a part of God itself. Actually the life is immortal. This creature of the life is conscious, pious and naturally pleasant. And that part of God, life has come under the influence of maya. It is tied like a monkey. People dance like a monkey with the influence of maya.

सो माया वस भयउ गोसाईं, बंध्यो कीर मरकट की नाईं॥
So Maya vas bhayau gosai, bandhyo keer market ki nayi.

Now Garud asked seven questions with Bhushandji and requested him to answer them in brief. Garun said: First of all please tell me which form of body is hard to be get. Which is the greatest sadness and the greatest pleasure in the world? What is the difference between saint and demons. Please tell me their nature in brief. What are the good deeds and what is the painful sin? You know every thing so please tell me what are the mental diseases. Now Kagbhushandi spoke gently that I shall tell you all the answer in brief. Please listen? There is no form of body like human being because all the creatures require this. The human body is superior than all.

नर तर सम नहि कवनिउ देही।
जवि चराचर जाचत तेही॥
सो तनु धरि हरि भजहि न जे नर।
होहि विष्नय रत मंद मंद तर॥

Nar tar sama nahi kavinau dehi.
Javi charachar jachat tehi.
So tanu dhari hari bhajahi na je nar.
Hohi vishay rath mand mand tar.

Poverty is a curse, so it is most painful thing in the world. To meet with the gentlemen or the saint is the pleasant thing in the whole world.

नहिं दरिद्र सम दुख जग माहीं।
संत मिलन सम सुख जग नाहीं॥

Nahin daridra sama dukh jag mahin,
Sant milan sama sukh jag nahin.

Non-violence is the greatest religion in the world. To insult the others is a great sin. Please listen about the mental diseases by which people get a lot of pain. Affection is the route of all the diseases because they create many infections. In this way all the creatures of the world are suffering from mental diseases. All the worldly creatures feel sorry, they feel pleasure, they feel frightened, they fall in love with worldly things and they feel sad when they are apart from their lovely things. The mental diseases which I have told are found in all the worldly creatures. All these diseases can be routed out only by the grace of Lord Sri Ram. Thus, all the Vedas and Puranas tell us that no one can get pleasure without the devotion of Lord Sri Ram. Kagbhushandji says to Garud that all the saints have also adopted the path of devotion.

सब कर मत खगनायक एहा, करिय राम पद पंकज नेहा।
श्रुति पुरान सब ग्रन्थ कहाहीं, रघुपति भगति बिना सुख नाहीं॥

Sab kar math khagnayak yeha, kareya Ram pad pankaj neha.
Shruti puran sab granth kahahin, Raghupat bagati bina sukh nahin.

Kagbhushandi told Garud, "It may be possible that oil can come out by crushing the sand and butter can come out by mixing the water. All these impossible things can become possible but without the devotion of Lord Sri Ram, no one can get moksha. This is the firm principle in itself."

वारिमथे घृते होइ बरू, सिकता ते बरू तेल।
बिनु हरि भजन न भव तरिये, यह सिद्धान्त अपेल॥

Vaarimathe grith hoi baru, sikta te baru tel.
Binu hari bhajan na bhav tariye, yeh siddhanth apel.

In this way the person who remembers Lord Sri Ram at every moment, they can face all kinds of difficulties by a little effort. Kagbhushandi further says that whatever I have told you about the character of Lord Sri Ram, that all is on behalf of my self experience and self thinking. Rishi Vyas has also told me in concern to Sri Ram. He said, "Well Garud this is the only principle that, please worship and remember Lord Sri Ram leaving all of the important work aside. Devotion in life and life is for devotion."

श्रुति सिद्धान्त इहइ उरगारी।
भजिय राम सब काज बिसारी॥

Shruti siddhanth Ihaye urgari
Bhajiya ram sab kaaj Bisaari.

Bhushandi said to Garud that you are the centre of wisdom and knowledge. Thus, you have bestowed your mercy on me that you have visited my ashram. You have asked me to tell the pious story of Lord Sri Ram which is pleasant to Suk-Sankadi and Lord Shiva. It is very hard to get the company of saints and sages. Well, please Garud, you see me, I am a crow. I have taken birth in the worst rank in the group of birds. But by the grace of God, I have become world fame pious. I have achieved the authority to worship Lord Sri Ram. Kagbhushandi said to Garud that, "Today I am very very thankful of Lord Sri Ram that he has given me a chance to get the company of great saint like you. You are the nearest and dearest of Lord Sri Ram. So there is nothing as secret for you. Whatever I have told you, this all is according to my own thoughts and experience. But the fact is that nobody can understand the secret character of Lord Sri Ram without his mercy. His mercy is unbound and unlimited.

> नाथ यथा मति भाखेउँ, राखेउँ नहिं कछु गोइ।
> चरित सिन्धु रघुनायक, थाह कि पावइ कोइ॥

Nath yatha mati Bhakheun, Rakheun nahin kachu goyi.
Charit sindhu Raghunayak, thah ki pawai koi.

Hearing the pleasant words of Bhushandi, Garud raised his feathers high in the sky. With the grace of devotion, all his illusion and delusion went away. He spoke gently, "Now I am very thankful by listening to your words which are mingled with the juice of devotion of Lord sri Ram. Now my all worries have gone away, which are under influence of Maya. I have become a great devotee of Lord Sri Ram. I may give you nothing in return, so I bow my head in your feet again and again. You are the most peace-loving personality in the whole world. You have a great devotion in the feet of Lord Sri Ram. You are beyond the influence of all the worldly worries, which is called maya."

Kagbhushandji said that, the saints, the trees, the rivers, the mountains, the earth, the sun, the moon and other stars are made by the nature to co-operate and serve each other. all these works are for the welfare of others, He further said that, the heart of a saint is like butter. But as far as I think the poets could not describe the dignity of the saints in a satisfactory way. On actually speaking, the fact is that, "The butter melts when it is being heated. But the person who feels sad in others' pains, he is only pious and true saint."

> संत हृदय नवनीत समाना, कहा कविन्ह पर कहइ न जाना।
> निज परिताप द्रवइ नवनीता, पर दुख द्रवइ संतसु पुनीता॥

Sant hriday navneet samaana, kaha kavinah par kahai na jaana.
Nij paritap dravai navneeta, par dukh dravai santasu puneeta.

Thus, my life has become thankful, because of your co-operation, all of my suspense has gone away. In this way bowing their head in the feet of Kagbhushandji the wise Garud went away to heaven pleasantly. Now his delusions have gone away with the influence of devotion.

Lord Shiva says to Parwati that it is very hard to get the company of the saints and sages. Even the Vedas and Puranas say that, without the mercy of Lord Sri Ram, it is total impossible to get the company of saints and sages. He said that I have told this pious story of God. And hearing this the fear of bhawasagar ruins automatically. The sin, which has been done by anybody in his life it is ruined, by hearing this story by heart.

The persons who hear this story by heart with faith, gets the devotion of Lord Sri Ram with a little effort, which is beyond the reach of the saints and sages also.

Only that person is wise, virtuous and world fame genius, whose mind is mingles and filled with the devotion of Lord Sri Ram. He is the only religious man, who follows the footprints of Lord Sri Ram. That country is thankful, the land is thankful, where the pious river Ganga flows. Nobody can describe the dignity of Ganga Mata. It is our faith that all our sins are washed away on taking bath in this pious river. So it is called Ganga Mata. That women are also thankful who follows her husband by body, mind and soul. That king is also praiseworthy who follows well his principles. That very Brahman is also worth praising, who never goes against his religion. That time of life is also thankful and precious when anyone gets the company of good gentlemen. That is called "Satsang". To take birth in the home of a devotee is also a matter of good luck. Lord Shiva says to Parwati that the family which produces the devotees or which gives birth to the devotees of Lord Sri Ram is also thankful and praiseworthy.

Kagbhushandji said, I have told you this story according to my reach and thoughts. Though I had made it secret at first. But by seeing your great live in the feet of Lord Sri Ram, I have told you all without my hesitation. This story should not be said to those rude persons, who did need for these things. It should not be said to those also, who are greedy, sexy and angry minded and to those also, who do not remember the God, the almighty, the father of the whole world and the creator of the universe. Only those persons are worthy to listen "Sri Ram Katha" who are fond of having the company of saints and sages. This story is more pleasant to those who love Sri Ram more than their life. In this way, the persons who want to have the devotion in the feet of Lord Sri Ram and want to get Moksha, they ought to listen to this story by body, mind and soul.

राम चरन रति जो चह, अथवा पद निर्वान।
भाव सहित सो यह कथा, करउ श्रवन पुट पान॥

Ramcharan rati jo chah, athwa pad niavran.
Bhav sahit so yeh katha, karu shravan put paan.

At last Lord Sriva says to Parwati that I have described the story of Lord Sri Ram in brief, which washes the brain of the people and which removes the mental dirtiness of Kaliyug. On actually speaking Ram Katha is Kalimal haran.

राम कथा गिरिजा मैं बरनी।
कलिमल समनि मनोमल हरनी॥
Ram katha Girija main barani
Kalimal samani manomal harani.

    The Seven steps of this pious book, the seven Kands of Sri Ram Charit Manas are the way route to get the devotion of Lord Sri Ram. the special mercy is poured on those persons, who keep their steps on these stairs, which will take them towards their goal - the devotion. The persons who sing this story by heart, their wishes are fulfilled by Lord Sri Ram. hearing all these stories, Girija (Parwati) became very pleased and said, "O Lord! By your mercy, my all delusions and suspense has gone away. Now the devotion of Lord Sri Ram has increased in my heart and mind. There are no troubles and worries in my mind."

    Thus, Goswami Tulsidas says that this very discussion of Lord Shiva and Parwati is the main source of heavenly pleasure. It ruins all kinds of worriness of the mind. It is the good means of recreation also. It is more lovable to the gentlemen. The persons who are the devotees of Lord Sri Ram, like it so much. Thus, in Kaliyug, there is no other means of devotion like yoga, yagna, penance and worship. So one should always remember Ram, he should always recite and listen the virtues of Lord Sri Ram. On actually speaking, Ram-Nam is only Bhawa Tarak. So Ganika, vulture king Jatayu, Azamil, the hunter, the elephant (Gajraj) all the great sinners have achieved Moksha by remembering Ram-Nam.

    Tulsidas further says, it is the blessing of Lord Sri Ram, that being the dull minded person I have also achieved most pleasures of devotion. So there is no comparison of Lord Sri Ram. He says that there is no poor man in the world like me, and He is the only helper of all the poors. So O Lord Sri Ram! Only you can help me to escape from the great pains of Bhawasagar. About Bhawasagar, it is imagined that the people have to go across very wide ocean after death, which is full of several types of troubles and difficulties. After death only our good deeds remain with us. Thus only our good deeds could help us to cross this troublesome ocean, the Bhawasagar. If someone has not done any good deed, he has always cheated the people, he has never donated anything to others, then, he will have to dive up and down in that very ocean, the Bhawasagar. And on the other hand, if anyone has done good deeds in his life, he has donated several good things to the poor and Brahmans, he has helped the needy persons, he has spoken the truth throughout his whole life, who has always followed the right path of religion, who has served their parents by all sides, only that person can go across this Bhawasagar very easily. Though this ocean is full of troubles and pains, so people call it Bhawasagar. Here Bhawasagar means the place of sadness and sorrows.

The fact may be this that Bhawasagar is the only matter of imagination. Nobody has seen it. Even then no one can describe it. What is the fact about the Bhawasagar, God knows. Whether there is any such type of ocean or not no one has seen it. Suppose if anyone has seen it, then he may not tell to others about their experience, about their sufferings and pains because he is no more in this world. He has left this world forever. So how he can describe about his sufferings of Bhawasagar.

In this connection as far as I think and according to my reach, can say that Bhawasagar is only the matter of imagination. In our daily life, we see that we get the same return what we do. If we do good for others, if we help others, if we always seek the truth, if our behaviour is polite to our elders and younger, if we are the devotee of God, if we are following the right path of religion, if we are of helping nature, if we are taking part in others' pains and if we are thinking for the good of the society, there is no doubt that the response will be good for us. There result will be this that our life will become easy and pleasant. We will enjoy all the heavenly pleasures on this earth. It means we have crossed the worldly sea, the Bhawasagar without any trouble. Our good deeds have helped us in every sphere of our life.

On the other hand, we see that our deeds stand before us like our shadow. If we have not done good for others, if we have not helped who are needy, if we have not given food to the hungry, if we have not donated good things to the poors and Brahmans, if we have crushed and pained the people, if we have killed thousands of men and animals, if we have been sinner the whole life and have done our work against the religion and if we have never shown faith in the existence of God and Godly creations, it is fact that we have to suffer in many ways. It is dead sure, it is certain that no one can escape us from different type of troubles which will come on behalf of our deeds. Only our deeds are our companion.

Thus, this world is Bhawasagar in itself. So if we have done good deeds, we will pass our life in a easy going way. We will pass our life pleasantly. It means we have crossed the Bhawasagar pleasantly without any pain. And if our deeds were not good, our life becomes troublesome. We get and we feel different types of pains. Several types of diseases gather us. Our family members, our relatives, our friends, begin to hate us. We don't get any type of support from any side of the society because we have never given food and water to anyone. We live naked in bitter cold nights of the winters because we have not donated or given clothes to needy persons. We do not get any better response from the society because we have never done any good deed for anyone. So the fact is that the response will be the same. If you have never saluted anyone, then who will salute you. In this way, the evil doers suffer from all these worldly pains. This very world, which we see by our naked eyes, is Bhawasagar. The evil doers dive up and down in this sea, while the gentlemen cross this Bhawasagar very easily. In this way our deeds accompany us. If we do good, the response will be good. If we will not do good, the response will go in opposite.

At last Goswami Tulsidas requests to his Lord Sri Ram to become so lovable for him as the beautiful lady is being loved by all and the greedy people love their wealth more than their lives. In the same way, you my Lord Ram, Please reside in my heart. In this way the persons who worship and remember Lord Sri Ram with body, mind and soul, get rid from all the worldly pains and troubles.

Sri Ram Charit Manas is the destroyer of all the mental disorders of Kaliyug. Now it ends.

Life History of Goswami Tulsidas

Birth Place

The founder of Indian culture, our great poet Goswami Tulsidas, was not a mere poet but also a great social reformer. It is considered that he was born on Samvat 1589. There are three factors about his birth place. Some people say that he was born at village Rajapur in Banda district of Uttar Pradesh. Others say that he was born in the district Ata at Soro. Some people say that Barah Kshattra in Gonda district is his birth place. Village Rajapur of banda district is mostly considered as his birth place. Now-a-days Bara Kshattra on the bank of the river Saryu of Gonda district is considered as his birth place. At present some important saints having their experience of life are trying to prove finally the birth place of Sri Tulsidasji as Barah Kshattra of Gonda district.

Goswami Tulsidas was born in a Brahman family. His parents left him forever in his childhood. According to Kavitawali:

मातु पिता जग जाइ तज्यो, विधि हूँ न लिखी कछु भाल भलाई।
बोर ते ललात बिललात द्वार द्वार दीन।
चाहत हो चारि एल चारि ही चनक को॥

Matu pita jag jaye tajyo, vidhi hoon na likhi kachu bhal bhalai.
Bhor te lalat bilalat dwar dwar deen.
Chahat ho chari phal chari hi chanak ko.

These statements are indicating that he passed his childhood in troubles. It was a matter of chance that a such type of orphan got shelter at the feet of Guru Narharidas. By the grace of Guru Narharidas, he got a chance to study Vedas, Puranas and other pious and religious books. After sometime Tulsidas went to Kashi with Swamji, who taught him Vedas and Vedant, Philosophy, History and Puranas.

Parentage

His father's name was Atmaram Dube and mother's name was Tulsi. In childhood Guru Narharidas nourished this orphan and preached him, told him the story of Sri Ram and taught Sanskrit. He studied in Kashi and was married to Ratnawali, the daughter of Deena Bandhu Pathak. Emotional hearted, Tulsi was much influenced with the charming face of his wife Ratnawali. Tulsi forgot himself. He forgot everything of the world. Actually, Ratnawali was a virtuous lady. When she saw that her wise husband is affected with her charm, she cursed and criticised him not by heart but by tongue and said:

अस्थि चर्म मय देह मम, तासो ऐसी प्रीति।
या आधी रघुनाथ सों, तौ न होति भव भीति॥
Asthi charma mayae deh mama, taso aesi priti
Ya aadhi Raghunath so, tau na hoti bahv bhiti.

When Goswami Tulsidas heard these words from Ratnawali, he awakened from the day dreams. His inner eyes were opened. He thought that all these worldly things are temporary. Nothing is durable in this world. So he left the world and was merged with Sri Ram. He roamed at every place of pilgrimage of India. Now he was fully devoted to Sri Ram. He began to recite the character of Ram in a poetic way. Thus, Tulsi became the centre of honour and devotion of everyone. In Samvat 1680, this great man left this mortal world forever.

संवत सोलह सौ असी, असी गंग के तीर।
श्रवण शुक्ला तीज शनि, तुलसी तजयो शरीर॥
Samvaht solah sou asi, asi, gang ke teer.
Shravan shukla teej shani, tulsi tajyo sharir.

His Writings

Sri Ram Charit Manas, the great epic is the symbol of Indian culture, religion, philosophy, devotion and poetic art. It is a media which highlights the virtues and abilities of Tulsi. Vinay Patrika highlights the poetic career of Goswami Tulsidas. It is written in Brij dialect, whereas Manas is written in Awadhi dialect. He also wrote Kavitawali, Dohawali, Gitawali, Barvai Ramayan, Ram Lala Nahchhu, Ramaggya, Prashnawali, Vairaggya Sandipani, Jaki Mangal, Parwati Mangal, Hanuman Bahuk, Krishna Gitawali, etc.

Goswami Tulsidas started to write Sri Ram Charit Manas on Samvat 1631 at the age of about sixty. He finished this writing in two years, seven months and twenty-six days. All the seven kands were completed on 1633 at the wedding day of Lord Sri Ram. Goswami Tulsidas went to Kashi on the order of Lord Sri Ram. He told Lord Shiva and mother Annapurna, the story of Sri Ram Charit Manas. In the night, the book, Manas was kept in the grand temple of Lord Shiva. In the morning, when the gate was opened, it was found that Satyam-Shivam-Sundaram is written on the book. It was marked by Lord Shankar. At that time, people heard the voice of Styam-Shivam-Sundaram from their ears.

On the other hand, when the Pandits heard about his, their hearts were filled with prejudice. They began to criticise Tulsidasji. They also tried to ruin that book. they sent two thieves to steal the book. The thieves saw that two brave men with bow and arrow are guarding the cottage of Tulsidas. They seemed very handsome. The evil thoughts of the thieves were washed away. Their mind became pious. They left stealing from that time. They became the devotee of Lord Sri Ram.

When Tulsdidas came to know that Lord Sri Ram felt trouble for him, he left all the things of his cottage and kept the book at the residence of his friend, Todarmal. After sometime, he wrote second edition. On the basis of the second edition, other copies were prepared. The advertisement of the book took expanse day by day.

The Pandits were not satisfied yet also. They thought a plan to take test to the book. In the temple of Bhagwan Vishwanath, above all they kept Veda, then Shastra then Purana and after all, Ram Charit manas was kept. Now the doors of the temple were closed. Early in the morning, when the temple was opened, the people saw that the Manas is above all. Now the Pandits were much ashamed. They begged pardon from Tulsidas. They touched and washed the feet of Goswami Tulsidas and drank that water with devotion.

Now Tulsidasji began to live on Assee Ghat in Varanasi. With the suggestion of Hanumanji, Goswami wrote Vinai Patrika and presented it in the feet of Lord Sri Ram. It is said that Lord Sri Ram himself made his signature on Vinai Patrika. Thus tulsidas began to lead his life in worshipping Lord Sri Ram.

On Samvat 1680, Shrawan Krishan Tritiya - Saturday at Assee Ghat of Varanasi, Goswami Tulsidas left this world forever.

Though Goswami Tulsidas is no more today but due to his writings, people remember him even today.

Specially, Sri Ram Charit Manas made him so great. There is no rival of this writing. Actually Manas is the gist of all the great books of the world. All type of teachings and preachings are found in this book. Fact is that every line of Manas is as effective as Mantra.

Mantra Maha Mani Visham byal ke.
Matat Kathin Kuank bhal ke.

Description Of Saints In Manas

The heart of a saint should be as soft as butter. According to Goswamiji, the butter melts on getting heated. But the heart of a saint melts when he sees anyone in misery and trouble. Others' sadness is the sadness for saint himself. The saint has a very wide heart. They always think for the welfare of the society as well as of the nation. the saint never feels proud of himself. Because they know well that the proud is the diet of God. The saints believe in simplicity. They mostly pass their time in devotion of God. Every citizen pay great regards for saints. It is our feeling that the saint is the photostat of God. This is why he has some extraordinary power. Tthe glimpse of his face attracts everybody towards him. At present we are breathing in twenty-first century. Even today, the saint is getting great regard in every religion. The Muslims, the Christians, the Persians, the Russians, the Japanese pay great regard and honour to the saints as well as the Hindus of India.

The fact is that the saints dedicate their lives for the development of the society. They always roam in the society. During this time they preach the people for their deeds. People consider their preachings and teachings as the message of God himself. They ask us not to tell a lie, because telling lie is the greatest sin in the world. They guide us what to do and what not to do. They put a clear interpretation of Paap (sin) and Punnya (good deeds). They show us the path of wisdom. Actually physical power is nothing. Only wisdom is power. If we are wise, if we have some reasoning power, if we have thinking capacity, only then we can escape from evils and bad deeds. To get knowledge is the first step towards our ambition, our goal, our aim of life. Eat, drink and be merry, may be the aim of those people who are belonging to the western culture and civilisation. But according to our Indian culture, this is not the aim of our life. Here our saints differ in thoughts from western thoughts. Our aim of life is something extra. According to Veda, Purana, Upanishad, Shastra and Shruti our aim of life is to get Moksha. The imagination about heaven and hell are the pillars of our religion. Our good deeds carry us to heaven and our bad deeds take us towards the hell. So it is the matter of our own thinking that we want to go to heaven or hell. This distinction can come in our minds only then when we have education and knowledge.

In this way the saints are getting the same regard in our society as Ganga, Gita, Gayatri, temple and cow. Goswami Tulsidas says in Manas that generally God comes on earth in the form of a saint. So who is actual saint and who is God in the form of a saint, it is hard to chalk out for us. Thus to get the blessings of God, we pay regard to the saints.

जो कोइ कहै संत हम चीन्हा। तुलसी कान हाथ दै लीन्हा॥
Jo koi kahe sant hum chinha, Tulasi kan haath day linha.

There are four Yugs. They are Satyug, Tretayug, Dwaparyug and Kaliyug. At present, we are breathing in the age of Kaliyug. According to the experiences of Goswami Tulsidas, the values and the regards of the saints will go down in Kaliyug. Because the persons of evil thoughts, the thieves, the dacoits, the evil doers, the criminals and the misbehaving people also may be seen in the form of saint. The persons who always goes against law and order adopt the form of saint to escape themselves from law. So at present the dignity of the saints has gone down in the society. People do not pay regard to the saints as before. Goswamiji says in Manas:

जाके नख अरू जटा विशाला।
सोइ तापस कराल कलिकाला॥
Jake nakh aru jata vishala,
Soi tapas karal kalikala.

We see that such type of people are generally found on religious places. They get success to befool, to cheat the innocent people. Thus, such type of people are the blot on the fair name of the Saint. We should try to recognise the dignity of the saints. According to my own opinion, if we follow the guide lines of the saints, our personal and social differences may finish. Because the saints never distinguish between a man and another man. In their eyes, no one is Hindu, no one is Muslim, no one is Christian, no one is Sikh. Everyone is a human being only. Thus ,they preach us to love the humanity. The saints must have a great place in our society.

जानहु संत अनन्त समाना।
Janahu sant anant Saman.

People of every caste, class, section and religion give more and more regard to saints and sages.

Ideals of A King According To Sri Ram Charit Manas

Ram Chandraji has presented an ideal as a king. After facing several type of difficulties, when Sri Ram Chandra became the king, he treated the subjects as his own sons. So every citizen was praising Lord Ram. Goswami Tulsidasji says in Manas that when Lord Ram was seated on the throne, everybody was very much pleased. With the grace of Sri Ram, people left all the family differences. There was no enmity among the citizens. According to Varnashram Dharam, everyone was doing his job. People were leading their life under the guidance of Shruti and Purana. They were loving each other. Everybody was fully devoted to Lord Sri Ram and thus, all were deserving to get Moksha. Without any disease, people were leading a long life. There was no poverty at all. Nobody was of ill health and virtueless. All the men and women were clever and virtuous. There was no cunningness at all. Everyone was wise enough. At that time Sri Ram was the only king throughout the whole world.

सप्तद्वीप सागर मेखला।
एक भूप रघुपति कोशला॥

Saptadvipa sagar mekhala
Ek bhoop Raghupati Kaushala.

Goswami Tulsidasji says that even mother Saraswati and Shesh Nag with thousands of mouths cannot describe the richness of Ram Rajya. People had great devotion in the feet of Brahmans. They were of a helping nature. The trees and plants were giving fruits and flowers in every season. Elephants and lions were living together in Ram Rajya. The creatures had also no enmity. They were also living happily with each other. The earth was always giving enough food to the people. All the rivers were giving healthy, clear and sufficient water. In Ram Rajya, the oceans were living under their limits. They were throwing the precious stones on their shores for the people. The tanks were always filled with clear water and a lot of lotuses.

In Ram Rajya, the sun was giving its heart according to the

need of the people. the clouds were also giving water with the demand of the subjects. Lord Sri Ram had done several great Ashwamedh yagnas He donated several precious things to the poors and the Brahmins. Being the mother of the universe, mother Sita was also serving Lord Ram with all of her efforts. Though she was the queen, no doubt, but she was independent on her feet. There were several servants in the palace, but Sita was doing herself all of her household duties. Sita was serving the mothers without any proudness. If our sisters of today may follow the footsteps of Mother Sita, there will be no quarrel in our houses. If they do not fight for their rights and if they only do their duties, well, many family differences may be finished. They can make their houses like heaven.

All the brothers were serving their elder brother Lord Sri Ram with simplicity. Ram had also great love for his brothers. He always used to preach and teach them about their formal duties. People were leading a happy and prosperous life in Ram Rajya. They were always requesting Brahma to maintain their devotion in the feet of Lord Sri Ram.

We all should take an example of brotherhood from Ram, Laxman, Bharat and Shatrughan. Ram left the throne for his younger brother Bharat and went to the forest. Laxman also left all the comforts of his life and followed Ram as if he could serve his brother in the troubles. When Bharat came to know that Ram had gone to the forest for him, he did not sit on the throne. He tried his best to content Ram but failed. And so he left all his princely dresses and comforts and lived in Nandi village for fourteen years. Bharat kept the wooden sandals of Lord Sri Ram on the throne and ruled under its guidance. Even then Bharat had decided that if Ram will not return to Ayodhya in due course of time, he will surely leave his life himself.

So if we follow the ideals of Laxman, Bharat and Shatrughan, all the burning problems of our society shall be finished. In these days everybody is standing for their rights. People are fighting for 'Chair'. Everyone wants to become a chairman. All the botherations are for chair only. But Bharat and Laxman had kicked the chair. So we should take an example from our ancestors and we ought not fight for the chairmanship. We should always be ready about our duties. We should be kind enough, as far as my thinking is concerned, if our present generation could follow the guidelines of Manas, if they could follow the footprints of Bharat, I am sure that there will be no quarrelling between brothers.

The problem of casteism may be finished if we see the friendship of Ram and Nishad Raj. The friendship of Sugreev, Hanuman and Vibhishan with Ram is an example for the humanity.

प्रभु तरूतर कपि डार पर ते किय आप समान।
तुलसी सीता नाथ सों साहिब सील निधान॥

Prabhu tarutar kapi daar par te kiya aap saman.
Tulsi Sita nath son sahib seel nidhan.

If we think it minutely, we will find that there is no comparison of Ram with Nishad Raj and Sugreev. Ram was the son of Dashratha, the mighty king of Ayodhya and Kewat was forest dweller. Sugreev and Hanuman were of Vanar race.

Although Vibhishan was of Rakshas race, yet Ram loved him dearly by heart. Sri Ram made them his friends. He embraced Kewat in his arms without any care of forward of backward castes, because there stands similarity in friendship. There is no question of haves or have nots. There is no question of poverty and richness. A real friend means the friend who helps to escape his friend from the sins and shows the path of wisdom. The real friend always thinks good of a friend. So Sri Ram has presented an ideal of friendship for the mankind.

In this connection it is my own idea that if we study Sri Ram Charit Manas minutely and if we follow the ideals of Lord Sri Ram, all the burning problems of the country may be solved very easily. When we will behave with others in a friendly way, then nobody will go in our opposition. Everybody will work in their own way. There will be no struggle for existence. People will give way to others for progress. Thus, the problem of untouchability, the problem of social differences, the problem of castism, the problem of forward and backward, the problem of haves and have nots, the problem of ups and downs shall be solved with a little effort. If we follow the teachings and preachings of Manas by heart, there will be no problem at all. In this way firmly we can say that every choupai of Sri Ram Charit Manas is a guideline for humanity. We realise this fact that Manas is beneficial for the mankind of the universe.

Dignity Of Guru In Manas

The word Guru is made of two words, that is Gu + Ru = Guru. Here Gu means darkness and Ru means light. Thus, the person who takes us out of the darkness towards light is called Guru. In this way Guru has a great importance in human life. The place of Guru is above all. Due to this Goswami Tulsidas has prayed his Guru in the beginning of Manas.

वन्दहु गुरू पद पदुम परागा। सूरूचि सुबास सरस अनुरागा।

Vandahu guru pad padam paraga, sooruchi subas saras anuraga

    Tulsidasji says that I pray the feet of my Guru, first of all whose essence of knowledge is interesting, tasty and charming for me. The effect of his kind mercy is as useful for me as nectar. His blessing is sufficient enough to ruin the pains of Bhawasagar. The toe nails of the Guru are shining like thousands of precious stones. Thus remembering the dignity of Guru, one can get extraordinary eyesight. And that natural light is enough to ruin the attraction and affection of worldly things.

    It is the grace of Guru Narharian which made capable Tulsidas to write Sri Ram Charit Manas. Guru Vishwamitra gave all type of education to Ram, Laxman in the forest. He made them perfect by all sides. Guru Vashistha also blessed and preached Ram, which made him so great. After getting victory on Lanka, when Ram came back to Ayodhya, his mothers asked him, "Ram my son, you are very tender in age and how have you killed mighty demon Ravana, the king of Lanka?" Ram gently answered his mother, "I have done nothing. It is the blessing of my family Guru Vashistha which has killed Ravana." Thus, the place of Guru is above all in the world. No one go across the Bhawasagar without the help of Guru. If a person who is most powerful like Brahma and Shiva, even then he has to get the mercy of Guru. Thus, Guru is the key point in making the personality.

Ramayan Ji ki Arti

Karo arti Ramayan Ji Ki
Glory virtue Siya Ram Ji Ki,
Chanting Brhama and Muni Narad,
Balmiki Scientist Visharad
Suk Sankadi Sesh and Sharad
Describing Hanuman morality. Karo arti Ramayan Ji KI... (1)

Singing Veda eighteen Purana
Six Shastra gist of all Grantha
Muni Jan Dhan, all of Santana
Gist of all, pious Granthan Ki. Karo arti Ramayan Ji Ki... (2)

Always singing sambhu Bhawani
Omnipotent Muni Vigyani
Byas and other poets have described
Voice of Kagbhushandi Ji Ki. Karo arti Ramayan Ji Ki... (3)

Ruining Kalimal, Worldly pleasure
Fine makeup youth lady ki
Finishing evils Bhawasagar nectar
By all means parents Tulsi Ki. Karo arti Ramayan Ji Ki... (4)

Karo arti Ramayan Ji Ki
Glory virtue Siya Ram Ji Ki
Karo arti Ramayan Ji Ki.

श्रेष्ठ विचार की उत्तम पुस्तकें

अभ्युदय
रामकथा पर आधारित वृहद् उपन्यास (2 खंडों में, मूल्य 400.00)

मर्यादा पुरुषोत्तम राम के जीवन पर आधारित इस उपन्यास में राम तथा उनसे जुड़ी महत्वपूर्ण घटनाओं का मनोवैज्ञानिक एवं मार्मिक विश्लेषण किया गया है। उपन्यासकार नरेन्द्र कोहली ने कई ग्रंथों की रचना की है पर अभ्युदय विशेष ग्रंथ है। दो खंडों में विभक्त इस उपन्यास के प्रथम खंड में दीक्षा, अवसर तथा संघर्ष की ओर - तीन उपन्यास तथा द्वितीय खंड में युद्ध भाग-1 एवं 2 शामिल किया गया है।

गलती किसकी?

अपने सार्थक कारनामों से हमेशा चर्चा में रहने वाली भारत की पहली महिला आई. पी. एस. अधिकारी किरण बेदी की लिखी पुस्तक 'गलती किसकी?' भला चर्चा में कैसे नहीं रह सकती, इस पुस्तक में किरण बेदी के व्यक्तित्व का दूसरा ही पहलू परिलक्षित होता है, बाहर से कठोर दिखने वाली किरण बेदी के कोमल मन का प्रस्फुटन इस पुस्तक में हुआ है। परिवार, समाज व व्यवस्था के शिकार हुए पीड़ितों का दर्द इस पुस्तक में आ साकार हो गया हो।

(मूल्य 95.00)

डाइनैमिक मेमोरी मेथड्स

यह पुस्तक लेखक के सात वर्षों के अध्ययन, अनुभव और शोध का परिणाम है। यह पुस्तक स्मृति उन रहस्यों को उजागर करती है, जो कई शताब्दियों के मानवीय प्रयास से खोजे गए हैं। साधारण व्यक्ति द्वारा समझी जा सकने वाली भाषा में यह पुस्तक प्राचीन ज्ञान और आधुनिकतम स्मृति-विधियों को संक्षेप में प्रस्तुत करती है जिससे सीखने की पूरी प्रक्रिया न केवल कुशल अपितु रोचक भी बन सके।

(मूल्य 60.00)

हिन्दू मान्यताओं का वैज्ञानिक आधार

हिन्दू धर्म में प्रचलित विभिन्न प्रकार की मान्यताओं का क्या कोई वैज्ञानिक आधार है? ऐसे ही गूढ़ प्रश्नों को उठाते हुए प्रसिद्ध ज्योतिषी डॉ. भोजराज द्विवेदी ने अपनी नवीनतम पुस्तक हिन्दूमान्यताओं का वैज्ञानिक आधार पुस्तक में 368 ऐसे ही प्रश्नों के तर्कपूर्ण उत्तर दिए हैं। जैसे- पाप क्या होता है? भक्ति किसे कहते हैं? इन सभी सवालों के जवाब पुस्तक में बड़े ही रोचक ढंग से दिए गए हैं।

(मूल्य 60.00)

पुस्तकें V.P.P. से मंगवायें। डाक व्यय प्रति पुस्तक 20/- तीन पुस्तकें एक साथ मंगवाने पर डाक व्यय फ्री। 1000 पुस्तकों की सूची निशुल्क मंगवायें।

◆ डायमंड बुक्स

X-30 ओखला, इंडस्ट्रियल एरिया, फेज-II, नई दिल्ली - 110020, फोन : 51611861 - 865, 26386289,
फैक्स : 011-51611866, 26386124, ई-मेल : mverma@nde.vsnl.net.in,
वेबसाईट : www.diamondpocketbooks.com

DIAMOND POCKET BOOKS PRESENTS
SHRI SATHYA SAI LITERATURE & SPIRITUAL BOOKS

Dr. S.P. Ruhela (Com. & Ed.)
- *Worship of Sri Sathya Sai Baba (In Roman) 40.00
- *World Peace and Sri Sathya Sai Avtar 60.00
- *How to Receive Sri Sathya Sai Baba's Grace 100.00
- *Sri Sathya Sai Baba : Understanding His Mystery and Experiencing His Love 60.00

B.K. Chaturvedi
- *The Miracal Man : Sri Sathya Sai Baba 60.00

S. Maaney
- *The Eternal Sai 40.00

Sushila Devi Ruhela
- Sri Sathya Sai Bhajanmala (Roman).............. 10.00

R.P. Hingorani
- *Chalisa Sangrah (Roman).. 40.00

Acharya Vipul Rao
- *Srimad Bhagwat Geeta (Sanskrit & English) 75.00

Dr. Bhavansingh Rana
- *108 Upanishad (In press) ... 150.00

Chakor Ajgaonkar
- *Realm of Sadhana (What Saints & Masters Say).......... 30.00

Dr. S.P. Ruhela
- *Fragrant Spiritual Memories of a Karma Yogi 100.00

Yogi M.K. Spencer
- *Rishi Ram Ram 100.00
- *Oneness with God 90.00

Eva Bell Barer
- *Quiet Talks with the Master 60.00

Joseph J. Ghosh
- *Adventures with Evil Spirits 80.00

K.H. Nagrani
- *A Child from the Spirit World Speaks 10.00

Religious Books in Hindi, English & Roman
- *Sanatan Dharm Pooja 95.00
- *Sudha Kalp 95.00
- *Shiv Abhisek Poojan 25.00
- *Daily Prayer (Hindi, English French, Roman) 25.00
- *Sanatan Daily Prayer 25.00

Acharya Vipul Rao
- *Daily Prayer 10.00

Dr. Bhojraj Dwivedi
- *Shiv Abhishek Pujan 25.00

B.K. Chaturvedi
- *Shri Hanuman Chalisa 30.00
- *The Hymns & Orisons of Lord Shankar 30.00
- *Chalisa Sangrah 40.00

Order books by V.P.P. Postage Rs. 20/- per book extra. Postage free on order of three or more books, Send Rs. 20/- in advance.

DIAMOND POCKET BOOKS (P) LTD.
X-30, Okhla Industrial Area, Phase-II, New Delhi-110020.
Phones : 51611861-5, Fax : (0091) -011- 51611866, 26386124